# the
# DALAI
# on WHAT
# MATTERS
# MOST

*Conversations on Anger, Compassion,
and Action*

## NORIYUKI UEDA

HAMPTON ROADS

WITHDRAWN

Translation by Sarah Fremerman Aptilon
Cover design by Jim Warner,
Cover art by Vipflash / shutterstock.com
Interior designed by Kathryn Sky-Peck

Hampton Roads Publishing Company, Inc.
Charlottesville, VA 22906
Distributed by Red Wheel/Weiser, LLC
*www.redwheelweiser.com*

Sign up for our newsletter and special offers by going to *www.
redwheelweiser.com/newsletter.*

ISBN: 978-1-57174-701-3
Library of Congress Cataloging-in-Publication Data available
upon request

Printed on acid-free paper in Canada
F

10 9 8 7 6 5 4 3 2 1

# CONTENTS

*Editor's Note for the American Edition* . . . . . *ix*

*Introduction: The Road to Dharamsala* . . . . . *xi*

ONE: What Can Buddhism Offer? . . . . . 1

*An Altruistic Society* • *What Matters Most* •
*A Biological Need* • *Cultivating Compassion* •
*Faith and Social Development*

TWO: Compassionate Anger . . . . . . . . . . 67

*Ritual and Meaning* • *Buddhism as "Science
of Mind"* • *Compassionate Anger* • *Good and
Bad Attachments* • *Knowledge and Practice*
• *The Dilemma of Modernization and Faith* •
*The Right Spirit of Competition* • *Emptiness
and Compassion*

THREE: Love and Attachment . . . . . . . 169

*Love vs. Attachment • Humans and Animals
• Love and Innate Healing Power*

FOUR: Enlightened Buddhism
for a Modern World . . . . . . . . . . . . . . . . 223

*The Buddha's Spirit of Social Service •
Self-Responsibility in Buddhism
• Transcending Suffering*

*Epilogue: After the Interview* . . . . . . . . . . . 261

*The Dalai Lama's Social Activism in India •
The Wings of Freedom • Salvation for All*

*Acknowledgments* . . . . . . . . . . . . . . . . . . . . 307

# EDITOR'S NOTE FOR THE
# AMERICAN EDITION

We have taken the liberty of editing the translated text of the Japanese edition in consideration of what topics would be most interesting and informative to a non-Japanese audience.

# INTRODUCTION: THE ROAD TO DHARAMSALA

I was thirty-one when I first heard the Dalai Lama lecture at an international conference in Bangalore, India. It was the fall of 1989, and I never imagined that in my lifetime I would be having a private interview with that great personality up on the stage. I had imagined him to be a solemn person, so I was amazed that the Dalai Lama who took the stage was so cheerful, open, and frank. The very next month he was awarded the Nobel Peace Prize. I felt that he was leading the world toward a better place.

For my generation and those that have followed, the Dalai Lama is a great spiritual celebrity. Always smiling, he expounds love, compassion, peace, and the spiritual awakening of every person. After he received the Nobel Prize, the Dalai Lama became a role model for the whole world. He is now summoned all over the world as a nonviolent leader and messenger of peace, and he has often engaged in dialogue with the world's political and religious leaders, with famous artists and scientists.

Few people, however, are aware of how turbulent the Dalai Lama's own life has been. In the spring of 1959, Chinese communist forces invaded Tibet and many Tibetans lost their lives. The capital, Lhasa, was occupied by China, and the twenty-three-year-old Dalai Lama was forced into political exile in India. When those events occurred, I was still an infant. For about as long as I have been alive, the Dalai Lama has lived in exile in India. For half a century, he has not been able to return to Tibet, and as the leader of its government in exile, he has called upon the Chinese government and the world to restore Tibetan autonomy.

From the time of the invasion of Chinese communist troops until now, it is said that over a million Tibetans have lost their lives. During the Cultural Revolution many Buddhist monasteries were destroyed, and because of the government's policy of massive immigration, Tibetans have become a minority in their own land. There is still no freedom of speech in Tibet today, and human rights violations such as detentions and torture are frequently reported. In September 2006, shocking images circulated on the Internet of Chinese troops who fired on and killed a defenseless Tibetan who had crossed the border from China into Nepal, an incident that drew international criticism.

The Dalai Lama, who has captured the hearts of so many people all over the world, who is a messenger of love, compassion, and peace, is the leader of the exiled government of a country where over a million of its people have been killed by another country's invasion, where the atrocities continue today. Even still, he is a leader who preaches love and compassion.

Since first seeing him in India seventeen years ago, I had not had the chance to see him in person again for a long time. Then in 2004, at an international conference in New Delhi, and again in 2005, when I had taken a position teaching at Stanford University, I was blessed with the chance to hear him lecture, and I was amazed. The Dalai Lama in person had a presence that couldn't be felt through all the books in the world. His gentle, disarming smile burned with a powerful energy. The Dalai Lama refused to allow his talks to be taken as insipid sermons about gratitude. He came across as a religious figure who was conscious that he was calling upon the world to act.

A month before this interview, at a Tokyo hotel where I was presenting a talk, I had the opportunity to ask the Dalai Lama for a meeting. "I believe that Buddhism has a big role to play in the world today," I said. "And I am impatient because Buddhists don't seem to realize that."

"That's right. Monks don't know about anything but Buddhism. In fact, they don't even know about that. They don't know about what they are doing, and many monks in Tibet also do nothing but perform rituals," the Dalai Lama said, laughing.

After we had talked for a little while, I hesitantly broached the subject that was on my mind. "Would it be possible for me to interview you? Please let me visit you in Dharamsala."

"Of course," he replied at once. "You're welcome to come to Dharamsala any time."

I had not stopped thinking about the Dalai Lama for a single moment since.

I want to eliminate war from this world. I want to stop the bullying of defenseless people. I want peace and happiness for all human beings. Since I was a small child, I have been captivated by this idea, even to the point of obsession, and I thought this time, meeting face to face with the Dalai Lama, I might find some kind of answer. I had no idea what an immense treat awaited.

—Noriyuki Ueda

[*One*]

# WHAT CAN BUDDHISM OFFER?

**UEDA NORIYUKI:** Your Holiness, I am very happy to have the opportunity to speak with you. For me it is a dream come true.

**DALAI LAMA:** I have also been looking forward to your visit.

**UEDA:** First I would like to briefly introduce myself and explain why I am here. I currently teach cultural anthropology and social reform theory at the Tokyo Institute of Technology, a leading scientific university in Japan. The goal of my main research interest, value systems, is to cultivate a new type of leader who combines expertise in the humanities and sciences and can cope with twenty-first century issues. The education of such leaders not only involves transmitting knowledge, but also strongly emphasizes debate.

In the hope of revitalizing Japanese society, I am also promoting what could be called a revival movement in Japanese Buddhism. Four years ago I founded the Buddhist Renaissance School as a place for dialogue and learning, and I serve as head of the school. I also chair meetings for "Monk, Be Ambitious!", a forum I created for dialogue, debate, and discussion of the future direction of Japanese Buddhism among young monks from all of its sects.

I feel that in my current activities, my childhood ideals are coming to fruition. For as long as I can remember, since I was about ten, I have been preoccupied with questions about why prejudice exists in the world, why so many people are starving, why people have to kill each other in wars. When I was young and thought about all the prejudice and violence in the world, I felt powerless. As one person among billions, I felt that I couldn't do anything. Now it seems strange to me that I felt so powerless at such an early age. I was an odd child who was preoccupied with social and political questions, yet at the same time I thought I lacked the means to do anything about them.

After I entered university, I got involved in a movement to help political prisoners, and I became a human rights and peace activist. But I had an experience at that time that was both shocking and depressing. The people who were working together as peace activists didn't get along at all. They attacked each other over their different definitions of peace. These people all wanted mostly the same things—to create peace in the world, to help those who could not defend themselves—yet they argued over minor differences in their definitions of peace, and they really hurt each other. I felt that this situation was hopeless, that it could never bring peace to the world.

DALAI LAMA: What was your group's definition of peace?

UEDA: At that time I belonged to a left-wing group, so we didn't think of peace merely as the absence of war. We defined peace as complete equality for all people. We sought to eradicate all injustice and prejudice. Later

I came to see this definition of peace not as a passive peace, in which the explicit violence of war would no longer exist, but as an active peace in which the structural violence of prejudice and poverty would no longer exist.

DALAI LAMA: I see.

UEDA: But even though we all shared a definition of peace as the salvation of defenseless people in society, whenever my colleagues found even small differences among their definitions, they argued and turned against each other.

I began to feel that there was something strange about these conflicts. I became aware that along with the external peace of social and political equality, there is also such a thing as inner peace. Even if I argue for peace, even if I act to bring about peace, if I myself am not peaceful, then nothing will come of it. If my heart is not peaceful, I will keep making enemies, and I will always be in conflict with others. The central question of my life became this: how to bring together outer and inner peace.

Now it seems strange to me, but at that time when I thought about inner peace and outer peace I never thought about Buddhism.

Even though I did two years of fieldwork in the Buddhist country of Sri Lanka, I felt that Japanese Buddhism was not only completely useless, but a sham.

DALAI LAMA: Exploitation.

UEDA: Yes. Buddhist monks preach compassion, but they don't really practice it. They talk about compassion and kindness, but they don't even notice those who are actually suffering or persecuted, and even if they do, they do nothing to help them. They preach Buddhist doctrine, but . . .

DALAI LAMA: It doesn't translate into action.

UEDA: Exactly. And they just repeat the same old rituals and get paid for it. They treat being a monk as a profession like any other, so you can't really call them religious people. That's how I saw them when I was in my twenties.

This was not only my opinion. Today in Japan many people see Buddhism in the same way. I feel that the Buddhist way of thinking is right; its temples and monks are the problem. The expression "funeral Buddhism" is usually used to criticize Japanese Buddhism, suggesting that all monks do is perform funerals and ancestral memorial rites. Most of those rituals are neither valuable nor truly religious, and some monks demand ridiculous amounts of money for performing them. The temples collect money from farmers, and the monks take it easy and get rich.

I have to admit that this view is somewhat biased. While many temples are wealthy, many others are poor, and many head monks have to take a second job to make ends meet. There are many wonderful, pure-hearted monks. But the many useless ones deserve to be criticized.

I believe in the potential of Buddhism because in the past ten years I have encountered many amazing monks and temple communities. These monks address the suffering that exists today. Monks who are struggling to reduce the suicide rate in Japan, where thirty thousand people commit suicide each year. Monks who are involved with hospice care for those suffering from incurable illnesses. Monks who are reaching out to older people and helping them plan their remaining years and how they would like to die. There are also monks who have opened their temples to young people who have lost hope, monks who take in delinquent youths and create a community for them. Their work extends beyond Japan—there are monks helping children who suffer from leukemia as a result of the Chernobyl nuclear disaster (which is important in Japan, because of the atomic bomb), helping neglected Thai AIDS patients, and dedicating themselves to the education of refugee children. Then there are those monks who might not be engaged in such visible activities, but who participate in conversations and events all over the world, and whose sincerity and character affect many people. These monks don't just preach compassion but also express it through their actions, and together they form the lively center of a global community. Their temples bring people together and offer support for each individual.

Yet Buddhist communities do not always value these deeply compassionate monks. They are seen as "merely" engaging in social activism, and their communities often feel that they should be involved in more "religious" activities. When you meet these compassionate monks, it is clear that they are not neglecting their religiosity at all. On the contrary, because they are religiously gifted, they cannot neglect those who are suffering. They are involved in these innovative activities because they believe in the possibilities for Buddhism.

In my interviews with Your Holiness, I would like to talk about how Buddhist teachings can relate to actual problems. I think there is a missing link between Buddhist doctrine and real social transformation, and I want to bridge that gap.

I would also like to discuss whether it is possible to construct an altruistic society, in which people take care of and help each other.

DALAI LAMA: I think your introduction was very interesting. This leftist or socialistic view is similar to my own way of thinking. The problem you describe is not easy to solve. It is not limited to Japan but is happening all over the world.

From a socialist perspective, we have to consider what kind of practical action we must take to solve this problem. Today there are two types of socialist system. The first type values freedom and democracy, as in the social democracies of Sweden and other European countries. The second type of socialist system is that of countries like the former Soviet Union and China. China actually is not a socialist system any longer. [Laughs.] Maybe North Korea. No, it couldn't be called socialist anymore either. [Laughs.]

UEDA: No one would call that socialism now.

DALAI LAMA: There is no hope for that type of socialist system. I think the socialist democracies of Europe are on the right track. They are not purely capitalistic, but individuals have the opportunity to make money, to make a profit. At the same time they take great care with social security and social welfare.

*I think the socialist democracies*
*of Europe are on the right track.*
*They are not purely  capitalistic,*
*but individuals have the*
*opportunity  to make money,*
*to make a profit. . . .*

*. . . At the same time
they take great care
with social security
and social welfare.*

# An Altruistic Society

UEDA: You often speak about creating an altruistic society that is full of compassion and kindness, and I also believe that constructing an altruistic society will become a major goal for humanity in the twenty-first century. It seems to me that an altruistic society is the one that can provide us with the most peace of mind. If those around me are altruistic and I get into any kind of trouble, I know they will be glad to help me. And if my friends have difficulties, I will be glad to help them. If a society is truly filled with kindness, then anxiety and fear will disappear.

DALAI LAMA: That's absolutely right.

UEDA: As I mentioned earlier, though, we live in a world largely governed by self-interest. And money. Because you are a member of a free-market economy, you should go to where you will be able to earn the most. Stop doing jobs for which you don't earn much, and do your best to find a job where you can earn a lot. Work that pays well is good work, and work that doesn't is bad work. By those standards, compared with the person who does work that benefits the defenseless members of society, such as a low-paying job taking care of the elderly, the person who earns ten times that by trading stocks or working in venture capital is considered the successful one, the great one.

In the market economy I am a piece of merchandise, so I am encouraged to sell myself for as high a price as possible. Because free-market competition determines whether or not I can sell myself at a high price, if I can only earn low pay, that is the result of competition, so it's my own responsibility. Then no matter how much I struggle, no one is going to help me. They'll say that this happened because I didn't make an effort. That's why each person must struggle to protect himself. If I run into trouble, no one is going to help me. In this way we are led to cling to selfish interests.

Many people are not happy with this self-centered worldview. Parents want to raise their children to be kind. The problem is, even if I am an altruistic, kind person, if my friends, colleagues, and the society that surrounds me are selfish, I'll be eaten up by everyone else. I will end up a victim of society, with others taking advantage of me. If society as a whole is altruistic, then it is easy for me to be altruistic. But if my social environment is self-centered, it is difficult. How can we overcome these circumstances to create an altruistic society and become altruistic, compassionate individuals?

DALAI LAMA: This is an important question. Creating a compassionate society, and a compassionate humanity, is my main objective. We need a more compassionate society because human beings are social animals. An individual's life and future entirely depends on society. If society is happier and more prosperous, then the individual will gain maximum benefit. That is a natural law. That is why, in any country, even if people are cheating each other, even if they don't have any genuine friendship, still somehow people prefer to live together. That's why we have big cities.

Everywhere in the world, people's lives are easier if they live together, so we create villages, towns, and cities. That is our nature. Individuals' interests and survival depend on their communities. I think that in so-called undeveloped regions, people are closer to this basic human nature than those

*We need a more compassionate society because human beings are social animals. An individual's life and future entirely depends on society. If society is happier and more prosperous, then the individual will gain maximum benefit. That is a natural law.*

who live in cities. For example, nomads or farmers who live in the countryside here in India may have a stronger sense of community. In the United States also I think there are big differences between those who live in cities and those who live in the countryside. The Japanese may be similar. There may be some differences between farm workers living in the countryside and those living in big cities, in terms of their sense of living in a social community. What do you think?

UEDA: That's true. In Japan too, people who live in the countryside are much more aware of community than those who live in cities. Modernization is advancing rapidly in Japan, yet in farming and fishing villages people still have a strong sense of community.

DALAI LAMA: So now the question is why these differences exist. In less developed areas, cooperation is more important. People help each other. There is more cooperation and more sense of community. For example, when someone dies, everyone gathers together and shares their sorrow. When we live in a society where cooperation is necessary, our awareness of ourselves as

*When we live in a society*

*where cooperation is*

*necessary, our awareness*

*of ourselves as*

*members of that society*

*becomes stronger.*

members of that society becomes stronger.

In big cities, each individual works in an office or a factory and receives his own salary. Each feels a greater sense of independence than those who live in a more cooperative society. Even if two people work together in an office or a factory, each fulfills his role and is paid accordingly, so each feels independent, and there is no sense of community. Each has the false impression that he works independently to feed himself, that he has his own salary, so there is no need to rely on others. Then even friendship just consists of social gatherings, smiling at each other, and

*We wrongly believe*
*that money is the most*
*fundamental thing in*
*human life.*

saying hello, but that's all. In a deep sense, each believes he is completely independent, but that is a false and superficial impression. This misconception alienates us from our basic human nature as social animals.

## What Matters Most

DALAI LAMA: In this way, we lose sight of our basic human values. Life is just based on money. We wrongly believe that money is the most fundamental thing in human life. The resource of money comes through skill and potential, but it is not based on altruism. We start to believe that money, rather than altruism or kindness, brings happiness. There is no system in which the genuinely compassionate person makes a higher salary and the cruel person makes a lower salary. No. [Laughs.]

UEDA: Just the opposite.

DALAI LAMA: Our society leads us to believe that our lives depend entirely on money, and money becomes the most important thing. This mistaken view also leads to educational

*We have the false impression that as long as we have plenty of money, we don't need compassionate friends or a compassionate society. I think that is due to a lack of understanding of our deeper human nature. . . .*

*. . . When you are in a desperate situation, money cannot console you. Only when another person expresses empathy and concern will you feel relieved and consoled.*

policies that emphasize not kindness, but the idea that making money is what matters most. We have the false impression that as long as we have plenty of money, we don't need compassionate friends or a compassionate society. I think that is due to a lack of understanding of our deeper human nature. As you mentioned, when an individual faces a personal problem, such as mental worry or unhappiness, then money cannot save him. Only affection and compassion can console him and make him feel calmer and happier. When you are in a desperate situation, money cannot console you. Only when another person expresses empathy and concern will you feel relieved and consoled.

UEDA: I don't have to mention Aristotle in relation to human beings as social animals. This is the essence of human existence, yet we have come to believe that society is not made up of people's connections to one another, but of money. That mistaken view is based on the illusion that anything can be bought with money. But as you said, it is clear that kindness and gentleness can never be bought. Why do human beings have this fundamental misunderstanding?

DALAI LAMA: On a basic level, human beings are mammals, but we also possess a sophisticated mind that sometimes creates false impressions and hopes, which leads us to act in mistaken ways.

Because other animals' minds are less sophisticated, they are much less likely to fall into this kind of mistaken view. If a dog was very ill, for example, even if you were to put some meat in front of him, I don't think he would appreciate it very much. Even if the dog were thin and needed food, if he was feeling sad, it would be better for another animal to lick him. That would be more effective.

Similarly, we human beings are animals at a deeper level, and we share the same physical needs as animals. Even a billionaire can experience sorrow, sadness, loneliness. At that time, even millions of dollars cannot show him affection. But when he has an emotional problem, if someone shows him affection and shares in his loneliness and sorrow, that will really help him. In this way we can understand the value of human affection. It is much stronger and more useful than money. When we are caught up in a false sense of confidence, we do not realize it. We think we are fine, that there is no problem. We

*Human affection is
much stronger
and more useful
than money.*

think, "I am healthy. I don't have any major problems. I'm a millionaire. I have plenty of money, and I can ask people to do whatever I want them to. I can buy what I want. Sometimes I can bully other people because of my economic power." But when that person faces real difficulties on an emotional level, then he realizes that his confidence in money was misplaced. It fails to provide mental comfort. We realize that our hope based on money was a false hope. That is the reality.

UEDA: I find that most people who attain this kind of realization are those who have experienced great suffering—facing death from a serious illness or having a business fail and going bankrupt. That is when a person starts to talk about how arrogant he was before, how anxious he was even when he was in a position of power, how ignorant he was about life and the world. Such experiences lead us to the edge of the abyss and teach us a new way to live, which is why we are often grateful later for the suffering we have had to face.

It might seem strange at first to feel grateful toward our own unhappiness and failure, but they lead us to a great truth. The value of the affection and kindness we discover in the process is so great that it is worth the price. As you said, that is the essence of human existence that penetrates the depths of our animal nature.

## A BIOLOGICAL NEED

DALAI LAMA: That's right. So the most fundamental issue is that since we are social animals, in fact what binds a society together are not laws, but affection and kindness. We are not forced by laws and rules to live together. We live together because of the affection that

*What binds a society together*

*are not laws,*

*but affection and kindness.*

*We are not forced by*

*laws and rules*

*to live together. . . .*

*. . . We live together*
*because of the affection*
*that naturally arises*
*within us.*

naturally arises within us. Affection is very effective for that purpose.

That is because we are social animals by nature. I always say that biological factors are crucial. From the moment of birth, a mother's affection is immensely beneficial to her child. And the newborn infant is totally reliant on his mother for survival. How do affection and kindness develop? Not because of religion, or education, or law, but because of biological factors. We need that affection in order to survive. That affection brings us together and creates communities. Affection does not arise from the compulsion of laws, or religion, or education, or money, but from our biological nature as human beings.

Therefore, we may think we are self-sufficient and independent, but deep inside we are still human beings who need affection. We cannot separate ourselves from these human values. By means of the true education that happens through investigation and analysis, we can reach the conviction that we need this affection to live. Even ordinary people who might not have this kind of sophisticated knowledge can confirm this truth through their own experience.

UEDA: I agree with you that the origin of affection and kindness is a biological factor that all human beings possess. I was also surprised that you have not yet mentioned Buddhism at all. In my experience, no matter what you ask a Buddhist, he will always reply that the Buddha said such-and-such, or he will refer to the teachings of the great master so-and-so and start preaching. But you never say that compassion, affection, and kindness are important because they are Buddhist teachings. On the contrary, these things precede religion, and they are true not for some religious reason, but because they are biological facts. I was amazed by your way of explaining this question.

If we pursue this topic further, it will lead into a discussion of Buddhism and its monks, and that will take us into different territory. So I hope we can talk about that later. For now, I will just say that I was very surprised.

## CULTIVATING COMPASSION

DALAI LAMA: Now let us return to your original question about how to build an altruistic society in today's world. You are concerned about Japanese society, so let's look at Japanese society. Japanese leaders and the population in general are well educated and have considerable material wealth. In that state, naturally they may not pay much attention to the importance of deeper human values.

Schools bear the responsibility for educating young people, but they do not do much to cultivate these values. From kindergarten through university, the intellectual aspects of education are treated as important, but the educational system never concerns itself with these deeper values. Cultivating these values is supposed to be the job of religion,

*A society that is based on money is aggressive, and those with power can bully and behave cruelly to others.*

*A society that depends on
money has problems that reflect
its beliefs.*

*In this kind of society, people
who value affection and
compassion
are treated like fools,
while those whose priority is
making money become
more and more arrogant.*

but religion has become so caught up in making money that it has become superficial.

The Buddha taught about the importance of compassion, but even though monks study these teachings, often they are not serious about what they are doing. They stop at an intellectual level and do not really practice what they have learned. I feel that our modern educational system fails to provide sufficient education about compassion. The time has come to transform this whole system. Society is formed through its educational system, but as you said, the educational system does not transmit the deeper human values of compassion and kindness. Then all of society lives with this false view that leads to a superficial life, in which we live like machines that don't need affection. We become part of that. We become like machines. That is because today's society is based on money. A society that is based on money is aggressive, and those with power can bully and behave cruelly to others. This situation produces growing social unrest. A society that depends on money has problems that reflect its beliefs.

In reality, affection and compassion have no direct link with money. They cannot create money. Therefore, in a society in which money is the priority, people don't take these values seriously anymore. As you pointed out a little while ago, people in positions of leadership, like politicians, have emerged from within a society that depends on money, so naturally they think like that and lead society further in that direction. In this kind of society, people who value affection and compassion are treated like fools, while those whose priority is making money become more and more arrogant.

# Faith and Social Development

UEDA: In a community that is filled with affection and kindness, even if people are materially poor they can be happy. I lived in Sri Lanka for two years, and I have visited Thailand many times. Even though many villages in Sri Lanka are materially poor, people help each other and share in each other's lives, and I have seen many examples of how they live happily in spite of their poverty.

I spent last year at Stanford University in California, in the heart of Silicon Valley, where many wealthy people live. Yet in spite of their apparent wealth, people there don't seem to be truly happy. Many suffer from stress and anxiety. Today they may have a lot of money, but they worry about tomorrow—they fear going bankrupt or broke, and they face the stress and frustration of living on a tight schedule. This reality raises complicated questions for me. Material wealth does not necessarily bring true happiness. On the other hand, while it is good to be happy in the midst of poverty, poor countries have big problems.

On a macro scale, we must bridge the gap between rich and poor. Buddhists with deep faith seem happy within their communities, yet in the wider world that gap keeps getting bigger. People who are filled with affection and kindness and are not swept away by material desires are getting poorer, while those who are frustrated and recklessly pursue selfish benefits instead are getting richer. What do you think about this point?

DALAI LAMA: That is a different factor. What I'm going to say now is not based on serious research, but is just something I thought up in my mind. Looking back at history, my rough impression is that in European countries around a thousand years ago people's lives were very difficult. . . . [I]n countries with warm climates like Africa, India, China, and other parts of Asia, . . . fruits and vegetables were available all year round. But European countries to the north had snow in the winter, so crops could only be grown in the summer, which made life extremely difficult.

Northern countries were also probably better off in ancient times, but as their populations gradually increased—in countries with little land area, like England, for example—living conditions became increasingly difficult. So they had to think about how to get more food from other lands. In the case of England, since it is a small island nation, food had to be brought by boat from other places. And then to acquire resources from these countries, they needed weapons. The warmer Asian countries had relatively small populations, and because of their climates, food was available all year round. So they had no need to acquire resources from other countries.

Europeans were forced to create technology because of their difficult climate conditions. They had to think about industrialization and technology in order to survive.

Countries like Portugal, Spain, England, France, and Belgium became colonial powers. These small countries became industrialized, obtained raw materials from other lands, used them to make products, and then began to sell those products back to other countries.

Asian countries, up to a certain period, did not have to worry as much about food, so they lived fairly peacefully. But then the imperialists came, and they lived under imperial rule, which became an obstacle to their development. Eventually part of the population in Asia received a Western-style education, adopted a Western way of thinking, and imported Western technologies, which led to trade with Western countries. In Asian countries, business had existed on a local level, but European colonization allowed it to expand to an international level. In Asian countries, one part of the population adopted Western ways of doing things and became rich, while those who still followed an ancient way of life remained poor. At a global level, the standard of living in industrialized nations rose to a much higher level than that of the exploited nations, and these nations became much more economically powerful. In those exploited nations, the few individuals who had the

" I hold the position
of a high monk,
a big lama.
Unless I exercise
self-restraint, there is
every possibility for me to
exploit others. "

opportunity to adopt a Western way of life became wealthy, while peasants and villagers who preserved the same lifestyle they had for thousands of years remained poor.

UEDA: One thing that particularly interests me is your use of the word "exploitation." This is the second time you've used that word, and I am surprised since it is a left-wing, Marxist term.

DALAI LAMA: It's true. I am also an exploiter. I hold the position of a high monk, a big lama. Unless I exercise self-restraint, there is every possibility for me to exploit others.

On my first visit to Mongolia, they arranged a tour to various institutions and a museum. At the museum, I saw a drawing of a lama with a huge mouth, eating up the people. This was in 1979, when Mongolia was still a Communist country. The Communists said that religion was a drug, and every religious institution was an exploiter. Even monks were exploiters. Even donations distributed to the monastic community were considered to be a form of exploitation.

When I came to the spot with that picture, the officials were a little bit nervous. I deliberately looked at it and I said, "It's true." Of course, I agree. I am not only a socialist but also a bit leftist, a communist. In terms of social economy theory, I am a Marxist. I think I am farther to the left than the Chinese leaders. [Bursts out laughing.] They are capitalists. [Laughs again.]

UEDA: That's true. [Bursts out laughing.]

[*Two*]

# COMPASSIONATE ANGER

UEDA: In the real world exploitation exists, and there is a great and unjust gap between rich and poor. My question is, from a Buddhist perspective, how should we deal with inequality and social injustice? Is it un-Buddhist to feel anger and indignation in the midst of such circumstances?

DALAI LAMA: This is an interesting question. Let's look at the matter first from a secular point of view. As I mentioned earlier, we should have more serious discussion and research about whether our so-called modern education system is adequate or not, in order to develop a healthier society.

Some American scientists I know are seriously concerned about social problems. Over the years we have had many discussions about the value of compassion, and several of these scientists conducted an experiment with university students. For a period of two to three weeks, they had the students practice attentive, deliberate meditation (mindfulness), and after the two or three weeks of meditation, they investigated what changes had taken place in their subjects. They reported that after this period of meditation practice, the students became calmer, had greater mental acuity and less stress, and had increased power of memory.

The University of British Columbia in Canada has created a new institution that is conducting research on how to cultivate warmheartedness in students within the modern educational system. At least four or five universities in the United States are acknowledging that modern education lacks something in this regard. Research is finally being conducted to address this problem and propose ways to improve the system.

Unless there is a worldwide movement to improve education and give more attention to ethics, this work will take a very long time, and it will be very difficult. Of course, in Russia and China the same dangers exist, and in India too. India may be a little better off because of its heritage of traditional spiritual values, even if they probably do not think about this question in terms of logic or reason. Japan is a modernized country and therefore Westernized, so Western problems are also occurring in Japan. With the adoption of a modern educational system, traditional values and family values have suffered. In the West, the power of the church and its support for the family has declined, and society has suffered the consequences. In Japan too the influence of religious

*Religion based on
faith alone can end up
as mysticism, but reason
gives faith a foundation
and makes it relevant
in daily life.*

*In Buddhism, from the start,*

*faith and reason must*

*always go together.*

*Without reason,*

*it is just blind faith,*

*which the Buddha rejected.*

institutions has faded, and with it, families have suffered.

Now let's talk about what role religious people can play in solving social problems. All religious institutions have the same basic values—compassion, love, forgiveness, tolerance. They express and cultivate these values in different ways. And religions that accept the existence of God take a different approach than those, like Buddhism, that don't. The current pope is a very sophisticated theologian, and though he is a religious leader, he emphasizes that faith and reason must coexist. Religion based on faith alone can end up as mysticism, but reason gives faith a foundation and makes it relevant in daily life. In Buddhism, from the start, faith and reason must always go together. Without reason, it is just blind faith, which the Buddha rejected. Our faith must be based on the Buddha's teachings.

The Buddha first taught the Four Noble Truths, the basis of all Buddhist doctrine, according to which the law of cause and effect governs all things. He rejected the idea of a god as creator of all things. Buddhism begins with the logical understanding that all happiness and suffering arises from specific causes.

*We must first be skeptical
and doubt everything,
as we do in the modern world.
Skepticism produces
questions, questions lead to
investigation . . .*

*. . . and investigation and experimentation bring answers.*

So Buddhism is rational from the start, particularly the schools of Buddhism based on the Sanskrit tradition, including Japanese Buddhism—that is, the Buddhism that carries on the great Nalanda University tradition from ancient India. According to the Nalanda tradition, everything should be understood according to reason. We must first be skeptical and doubt everything, as we do in the modern world. Skepticism produces questions, questions lead to investigation, and investigation and experimentation bring answers.

Buddhists do not believe the teachings of the Buddha merely because he expounded

*Buddhists do not
believe the teachings
of the Buddha
merely because he
expounded them.*

them. We approach the teachings with a skeptical attitude, and then we investigate whether they are true. Once we know that a teaching is truly correct, then we can accept it.

UEDA: I agree that Buddhist teachings are not mere mysticism, but are based on reason. But Japanese Buddhism has diverged considerably from that reason-based approach. For example, in Zen Buddhism, the goal is to transcend verbal logic. In the Nembutsu faith [of the Pure Land sects], the goal is to entrust ourselves completely to the saving power of Amida Buddha. Because Japanese Buddhists emphasize transcending logic and surrendering oneself, they tend to say that logical statements are not really Buddhist and to assume that people who think in a logical way have achieved only a low level of Buddhist understanding or have not yet completely surrendered themselves. When these Buddhists say things like, "Don't confuse yourself with logic. Just have faith," that gives monks an excuse to stop investigating their own experience in a rational way.

As you said, Buddhism begins with our own questions, and its core is the investigation of those questions. Among Japanese Buddhists,

*We approach the teachings
[of the Buddha] with a
skeptical attitude, and then
we investigate whether
they are true. . . .*

*. . . Once we know that a teaching is truly correct, then we can accept it.*

when you raise your own questions, people say that you don't have sufficient faith or that you haven't practiced Buddhism enough yet. As a result, many monks abandon the effort of thinking for themselves. To surrender oneself to the teachings of a sect's founder and believe in them absolutely, without doubting them, might at first appear to be an act that comes from a deeper faith-mind, but that act always contains the possibility of what we call blind faith. Not only that, but the blindly faithful end up discouraging young people who seek to investigate things for themselves. Because young people today doubt traditional teachings, ask serious questions, and seek to deeply investigate them, traditional Buddhism can offer them wisdom. If those questions are disregarded from the start, then the opportunity to deeply investigate Buddhist teaching is lost, and Buddhism can never become relevant for our time.

## RITUAL AND MEANING

DALAI LAMA: In that sense, we Buddhists are all the same. Just as in Japanese temples, in many Tibetan monastic institutions, the monks perform rituals without knowing any-

*In many Tibetan monastic institutions, the monks perform rituals without knowing anything about their meaning. . . . The ritual is just a means to earn money. They are not concerned about nirvana or the next life. . . .*

*. . . They only think about*

*how to earn money in this life.*

*If people make offerings,*

*the monks are happy.*

*The same situation also exists*

*in many Christian churches*

*around the world.*

thing about their meaning, and they have no desire to study Buddhist doctrine. The ritual is just a means to earn money. They are not concerned about nirvana or the next life. They only think about how to earn money in this life. If people make offerings, the monks are happy. The same situation also exists in China and in many Christian churches around the world.

UEDA: The same problem exists in Tibet?

DALAI LAMA: Yes, in some monasteries. [Turns to his English translator, Geshe Dorje

*If we only
practice Buddhism
at the level of ritual,
it can never help us
to solve today's
social problems.*

Damdul.] You know all about this, how monks who don't study are always performing rituals without knowing the meaning of the sutras. That is why ever since I went into exile in India, I have said over and over again that we must study the sutras. Whether we are Tibetan, Chinese, or Japanese, we should become Buddhists of the twenty-first century. If we accept our religion, we must understand its meaning. Then we become serious about our faith and practice. Otherwise it's just fashion.

Since my first visit to Japan in the 1960s, I have gotten the impression that monks perform many rituals, but do not pay much attention to studying Buddhist doctrine. University professors and scholars are the ones with the knowledge. Whether they are Buddhists or not, they have much more knowledge.

Fortunately, among Tibetan monks there are real scholars who possess broad and deep knowledge that comes from thirty years of study. People with blind faith will go to a temple when someone dies, and a monk will recite sutras. But if we only practice Buddhism at the level of ritual, it can never help us to solve today's social problems.

# BUDDHISM AS "SCIENCE OF MIND"

DALAI LAMA: To sum up, the most important thing is to promote human values as the foundation of daily life, through education.

I also think it is important not to think of Buddhism as a religion but as a "science of mind." Then it has greater potential to help promote basic human values. As a science of mind, Buddhist knowledge can be used to enhance secular education and thus help students develop the qualities of affection and kindness that human beings originally possess. Already in the West, scientists are beginning to make use of Buddhist techniques—not as a religion, but as a set of scientific techniques, such as meditation and the analysis of mind.

Traditionally Buddhism is divided into so-called Hinayāna ["Small Vehicle"] and Mahāyāna ["Great Vehicle"]. Hinayāna doctrine teaches us not to harm other living beings; Mahāyāna emphasizes not only not harming others, but also helping them. Therefore, when a Buddhist sees poverty or injustice, he should not remain indifferent.

In the Catholic Church in Latin America,

*The most important thing is to promote human values as the foundation of daily life, through education. . . .*

*. . . It is important
not to think of
Buddhism as a
religion but as a
"science of mind."*

some leaders are very concerned about social injustice, so they are leftists in that sense. When religious people get too involved in social activism, their work becomes political. What about in Sri Lanka? Japan? I have heard that in Korea some monks are quite active in the political realm. I don't know the details, but that's what I've heard.

UEDA: I think the debate is still unfolding about liberation theology, the church's political activities in Latin America on behalf of weak members of society. Either way, it is a great effort that we cannot ignore.

In Sri Lanka too, some monks get involved in politics. But in the ongoing civil war between the many Sinhala Buddhist sects and the few Tamil Hindu sects, political action can lead to Buddhism being linked to Sinhalese nationalism, so it's a difficult problem.

In any case, as you said, Hinayāna Buddhism is criticized as the "Small Vehicle" that makes individual liberation its goal and is focused on self-benefit, while Mahāyāna Buddhism developed with an emphasis on altruistic practice for the salvation of others, so its nature is fundamentally social.

# Compassionate Anger

DALAI LAMA: When faced with economic or any other kind of injustice, it is totally wrong for a religious person to remain indifferent. Religious people must struggle to solve these problems.

Here the issue is how to deal with anger. There are two types of anger. One type arises out of compassion; that kind of anger is useful. Anger that is motivated by compassion or a desire to correct social injustice, and does not seek to harm the other person, is a good anger that is worth having. For example,

*Anger that arises out of compassion is useful. Anger that is motivated by compassion or a desire to correct social injustice, and does not seek to harm the other person, is a good anger that is worth having.*

a good parent, out of concern for a child's behavior, may use harsh words or even strike him. He may be angry, but there is no trace of any desire to hurt him.

Japanese temples often enshrine the fierce manifestation of [the Buddhist deity] Acala. [Opens his mouth to make a face like an angry deity.] But Acala has that fierce expression not out of hatred or a desire to harm sentient beings, but out of concern for them, to correct their mistakes, like a parent's desire to correct a child's mistakes. As you rightly mentioned, anger brings more energy, more determination, more forceful action to correct injustice.

UEDA: Of course, it should be accompanied by compassion.

DALAI LAMA: Yes. The deep motivation is compassion, but it takes anger as the means to accomplish its ends.

UEDA: To use anger as a motivating force, should we transform it into another state, into something positive? Or should we maintain it as it is?

DALAI LAMA: The question is a person's state of mind or the motivation that causes

*If we act when our inner motivation is hatred toward another person, then that hatred expressed as anger will lead to destructive action. This is negative action.*

But if we act out of
consideration for the other
person, if we are motivated
by affection and sympathy,
then we can act out of anger
because we are concerned with
that person's well-being.

the action. When we act, that act arises out of a cause that already exists in us. If we act when our inner motivation is hatred toward another person, then that hatred expressed as anger will lead to destructive action. This is negative action. But if we act out of consideration for the other person, if we are motivated by affection and sympathy, then we can act out of anger because we are concerned with that person's well-being.

In this way, the parent acts out of concern for the children. If a child is playing with poison, for example, there is a danger that he may put it in his mouth. That is an emergency situation, and the parent may shout or strike the child's hands, but only out of genuine concern for him, to stop him from doing something dangerous. As soon as the child drops the poison, the parent's anger stops. That is because the anger was directed toward the child's actions that could harm him, not toward the child himself. In such a case, it is right to take the necessary measures to stop the action, such as anger, shouting, or striking.

If the anger is directed toward the person, if there is ill feeling toward the person, then that feeling will persist for a long time. When someone tries to harm you, or you feel that you have been harmed, then you have a negative feeling toward that person, and even if he is no longer acting in that way, you still feel uncomfortable toward him. In the previous case, as soon as the child's wrong action stops, the parent's anger goes away. These two types of anger are very different.

UEDA: What about anger toward social injustice? Does it last for a very long time, until the social injustice goes away?

*Anger toward social injustice will remain until the goal is achieved. It has to remain. It is necessary in order to stop social injustice and wrong destructive actions.*

DALAI LAMA: Anger toward social injustice will remain until the goal is achieved. It has to remain.

UEDA: I see. Should one truly continue to harbor a feeling of anger?

DALAI LAMA: Of course. That anger is directed toward the social injustice itself, along with the struggle to correct it, so the anger should be maintained until the goal is achieved. It is necessary in order to stop social injustice and wrong destructive actions.

For example, a negative or harsh attitude toward Chinese wrongdoing, such as human rights violations and torture, will remain so long as those actions continue.

## Good and Bad Attachments

UEDA: I am very impressed by what you said. Most of the Japanese monks I know who are engaged in various forms of social action are inspired by anger or indignation, but other monks often tell them that they are not yet enlightened and have only a low level of Buddhist insight. Japanese Buddhism teaches that regardless of whether or not anger is

*Buddhism teaches
that we must
overcome attachment,
but people often
mistake detachment
for indifference.*

based on compassion, we should suppress it. Even in the face of social injustice, even if terrible things are going on, to be angry is not Buddhist—it is an outrage against Buddhist doctrine. At the same time, many monks get angry about trivial things.

DALAI LAMA: [Points to his head.] I think we are talking about understanding on an intellectual level.

I once spoke to a wealthy Swiss woman who asked me about attachment. Buddhism teaches that we must overcome attachment, but people often mistake detachment for indifference. This woman thought that over-coming attachment meant not even acknowl-edging good things as good. For example, she asked me if the mind that seeks enlighten-ment is not attachment to enlightenment, and shouldn't we get rid of it? But the mind that seeks enlightenment is an attachment that we should keep, not discard. The attachment that seeks what is good is worthwhile.

This woman also said that without attach-ment she could not truly engage in altruistic practice. But that is also a mistaken view. I said that bodhisattvas have many attachments. The kind of attachment that we must discard is the desire that is based on biased views. The valuable desire of an unbiased heart is not the kind of attachment that we should discard. In Buddhism, to get rid of attachment means to get rid of misguided desires, but we still need valuable and good desires, and they should not be discarded. Valuable and good desires, such as the mind that seeks enlightenment, are not the mind of desire that Buddhism teaches that we must overcome. For the sake of realizing the good mind that has greater goals, such as enlightenment, we have to overcome the mind of attachment that has only small goals based on biased views.

*The kind of
attachment that we
must discard is the
desire that is based
on biased views. . . .*

*. . . The valuable desire of an unbiased heart is not the kind of attachment that we should discard.*

This idea may be difficult to understand since we use the word "attachment" to refer to both kinds of desire. But the mind that seeks good things such as enlightenment is worth keeping, while the mind of attachment based on biased views must be extinguished.

I feel the Japanese monks you speak of are not thinking about actual practice. In theory, it is true that anger is never good and we must get rid of all attachment. But when we actually confront social injustice and think about how to correct it, not all anger is bad, and we shouldn't try to overcome all attachment. Anger is bad in theory, and we must get rid of attachment, but in practice, we cannot completely negate them all. We must discern between theory and practice.

UEDA: What you just said about the two kinds of attachment really opened my eyes. I was always mystified by this question of attachment. In Japanese Buddhism, a small number of very influential Zen, Shingon, and other monks have said that they are enlightened and detached from material things, so even if they have several expensive foreign cars or Rolex watches, carouse with geisha every night, and spend incredible amounts of money, it's no problem because they are detached.

Any ordinary person would think this discrepancy was odd. They use the logic of overcoming attachment in Buddhism to justify their actions. These few monks' behavior has alienated many Japanese from the Buddhist faith and has made them think it is a waste of time.

To overcome attachment does not mean to become indifferent. Bad attachment should be abandoned, but good attachment should be maintained as we keep striving to improve ourselves.

DALAI LAMA: According to the Tibetan esoteric teaching of Dzogchen, when we undergo religious training, we have to have a correct knowledge of how to act and how not to act. As you said, these monks say they don't have any more attachments, while in reality they are enjoying many worldly things. They are supposed to have this inner understanding, yet they behave in a misguided way that reveals just the opposite. We have to express in practice what we have inwardly understood. They say they understand, but their actions show their understanding is false.

*The mind that seeks good things such as enlightenment is worth keeping, while the mind of attachment based on biased views must be extinguished.*

The practice of the precepts (Vinaya), which plays an important role in Buddhism, offers much practical advice. Zen and other "higher" forms of practice take mental understanding more seriously than they do physical actions in daily life, which they consider to be insignificant since these actions belong to a lower level of existence. I think Vinaya is not practiced very much in Japanese Buddhist monasteries. The same thing happens in Tibetan society. Many senior monks living in the United States say they have attained deep enlightenment, and that since they are engaged in such a high level of religious practice, it doesn't matter what they do. So they behave just like any worldly person. Of course, in Buddhist practice, no matter what a person has inwardly understood, he must keep the precepts, and that kind of behavior is evidence that one is not practicing the precepts.

UEDA: It is just as you say. In Japan, because spirituality is seen as so important, enlightenment is overemphasized, and we tend to disregard behavior in daily life because it is something that belongs to a lower level. The behavior of those monks I described says more about what kind of people they are than it does about Japanese Buddhism. But the fact that they exist and sometimes wield considerable authority in their communities does reflect problems inherent to Japanese Buddhism.

Of course, in Japan there are also many monks who deserve sincere respect.

DALAI LAMA: Of course.

# KNOWLEDGE AND PRACTICE

DALAI LAMA: In Tibetan monasteries there is a tendency for monks to study the meaning of the sutras, but not to calm their minds through practice. They gain knowledge, but do not practice it. Since ancient times, monks in the monasteries have studied the sutras and at the same time have been taught the system of Lamrim [or the "Great Exposition on the Stages of the Path," by Tibet's great scholar monk Tsongkhapa, 1357–1419], which focuses on calming the mind and transforming the personality. But recently

*The Buddha clearly taught*
*that even if one has*
*great knowledge,*
*if his mind is not quiet,*
*then the knowledge*
*is worthless.*

our monks focus more on the sutras and less on Lamrim. It depends on the master who is teaching, but if he is a great master, he will not only teach the sutras, but also good methods for calming the mind and improving oneself. If a master offers only knowledge, then no matter how much his disciple knows about the sutras, he may still be arrogant, jealous, and ignorant, and his mind will not be quieted. Those are signs that a person has gotten caught up in study without practice.

UEDA: That is true.

DALAI LAMA: The Buddha clearly taught that even if one has great knowledge, if his mind is not quiet, then the knowledge is worthless. Tsongkhapa composed a gatha (four-line verse) that says, "Even if one hears many teachings, if his heart is not calm, then he has not practiced them." When we receive teachings from a master, we should not accept them only on an intellectual level, but must take them to heart and use them to quiet our minds. In Tibetan monasteries monks learn not only to recite sutras, but also the teachings of Lamrim, so they take the meaning of the sutras into their own hearts and use them to direct their minds in a positive way.

## The Dilemma of Modernization and Faith

UEDA: Until now in traditional Buddhism knowledge was transmitted from master to disciple, with the master paying careful attention to the each stage of the disciple's learning and spiritual growth, and passing on only the knowledge and practice that were appropriate for that point in his development. Since ancient times, Buddhist education has been passed down from master to disciple in this flexible way. In Japan, some argue that Buddhist knowledge should not be transmitted in a formal setting like a university, outside the context of a master-disciple relationship, where it may be subject to serious misinterpretation.

DALAI LAMA: Some monasteries in Tibet are also becoming like universities. Some now go by the name "university." Of course, in their Buddhist studies programs they offer individual courses just as in any other university, but the difference between these institutions and ordinary universities is that their teachings usually emphasize that disciples must transform their own hearts through the teachings of Lamrim. They teach clearly which kinds of actions should be cultivated and which kinds should be overcome. These institutions may call themselves universities, but their approach sets them apart.

Tibetans in exile in India, however, go through the regular educational system, and fewer and fewer young people are now entering monasteries once they complete their secular education. [Turns to Geshe Dorje Damdul.] Young people who come straight from

Tibet and don't yet have a clear understanding of this situation probably do still enter the monasteries. What do you think?

GESHE DORJE DAMDUL: Recently many people have ended up migrating to the United States and other Western countries, and the number of monks who enter the monasteries to study Buddhism is dwindling. There is a danger that when they come out of the schools in the regular modern educational system, they will not be very interested in religion.

**DALAI LAMA:** What will happen if Tibet becomes a modern society?

**GESHE DORJE DAMDUL:** Certainly fewer and fewer people will enter the monasteries.

**DALAI LAMA:** If Tibetans adopt a modern educational system, and Tibetans' way of earning a living changes as a result, then monasteries may become mere academic institutions. That would be really dangerous for Tibetan society.

What should we do? We should put more energy into teaching Buddhism in schools. If we come up with a policy to incorporate the study of Buddhism in schools within the modern educational system as well, then those who come out of these schools will still have a knowledge of and interest in Buddhism, and some may decide to enter monasteries so they can transform their minds. For this purpose we must also create Buddhist universities and institutions where ordinary young laypeople, male or female, can go to study. If they all enter the monasteries and become monks and nuns, there will be far too many of them who should never have been there in the first place. [Laughs.] It is necessary to create such universities for young people who are interested in practicing Buddhism and polishing their minds as laypeople.

The Institute of Buddhist Dialectics in Dharamsala does not admit Tibetan women. This enrollment policy is now being debated, but no decision has yet been made. It should definitely be changed, so that laywomen will have a place to study Buddhism. Some Tibetan women who applied to study at the Institute of Buddhist Dialectics but were not admitted are now studying at the nunnery Jamyang Choling Institute. I have spoken with one of their teachers, the *geshe* of Loseling monastery [in South India], and I understand that these women are extremely gifted and passionate students of Buddhism. We must create institutions where women like this can study.

Of course, it would be difficult for monasteries to begin admitting laypeople, but all men and women, lay or monastic, should have places to study Buddhism. Parents who are well educated in Buddhism can pass on that knowledge and practice to their children. The Institute of Buddhist Dialectics admits foreigners, but is still closed to Tibetan laywomen.

# THE RIGHT SPIRIT
## OF COMPETITION

UEDA: All right. Returning again to the question of how to create an altruistic society, I want to ask you about the meaning of competition. More and more Japan is becoming a society governed by tough competition, which makes life very difficult. One problem is our desire to become this competitive society, but another problem is that those who criticize this competitiveness tend to emphasize only its negative side. But I believe that competition can also be very valuable.

DALAI LAMA: Right.

UEDA: I think there are two kinds of competition. First there is the kind that allows us to empower each other. For example, in martial arts such as judo and kendo, when two people compete, they are not caught up in winning or losing, but battle as rivals who enhance each other's strengths, which is a great thing. But nowadays in Japanese society, we have adopted the American type of competition that determines a winner and a loser. The result is that the winner takes all and the loser suffers, and no matter how difficult his life becomes he has to bear it, because he lost the competition. This kind of competition that produces a winner and loser, a winning team and a losing team, is becoming more prevalent.

I think the word "competition" can refer to many different kinds of competition. What do you think, Your Holiness?

DALAI LAMA: Yes, I fully agree. I also make a distinction between the good and worthwhile kind of competition that you describe and the other kind that is not. In the best kind of competition, we aim to accomplish a particular goal, and when we look at the good qualities

*In the best kind of competition, we aim to accomplish a particular goal, and when we look at the good qualities that others possess, we want to achieve the same thing for ourselves.*

that others possess, we want to achieve the same thing for ourselves. That kind of competition is positive. In Buddhism we say, "Take refuge in the three treasures of the Buddha, dharma, and sangha," and in a sense we feel a kind of rivalry with the "three treasures." We take the Buddha and sangha (monastic community) as our models, so that we can strive to attain a higher state. This kind of competition is positive and necessary for our development.

Then there is the negative type of competition that must be overcome, as you just said. This is the type of competition that draws a line and says, "I am the winner, and you are the loser." In this type of competition, we try to harm the other person and put ourselves first, and in that way we create our own enemy. The more prevalent this type of competition becomes, the more problems it creates in a society. But a positive spirit of competition allows us to lift each other up, to help each other, so that everybody ends up on top.

UEDA: That is very true. Last year I saw that in the United States competition is all about winning and losing. Even if I win today, I

*The negative type of*
*competition must be*
*overcome. This is the*
*type of competition that*
*draws a line and says,*
*"I am the winner, and*
*you are the loser. . . "*

*. . . But a positive spirit*
   *of competition allows us*
   *to lift each other up, to*
   *help each other,*
   *so that everybody*
   *ends up on top.*

might lose tomorrow, so the harsh reality is that my mind can never rest.

**DALAI LAMA:** Oh yes, China is the same way. In China, once you lose it's all over. [Makes a gesture of cutting his throat, laughs.]

**UEDA:** I think the same thing is happening in Japan. Until now, competition in Japan allowed us to inspire each other. We trusted each other and society. But the competition we now aspire to is the law of the jungle, the kind that determines a winning team and a losing team. We no longer respect or trust each other, and trust in society is also being lost.

## EMPTINESS
## AND COMPASSION

UEDA: This next question is related to something I asked you when I was in the audience at your lectures in Shinagawa and Hiroshima last year. It has to do with the connection between the understanding of emptiness and compassion.

The highest-ranking monks of the Shingon sect were all sitting in the first few rows of that large hall, which held about 800 people. In contrast to the laypeople and younger monks, who were sitting further back, listening to you with great enthusiasm, I was surprised at how apathetic those senior monks seemed. They sat there looking very relaxed, as though they were hardly listening. In the midst of all the excitement in the room, only their energy was lagging.

On that occasion you spoke repeatedly about the importance of compassion and kindness as the essence of Buddhism, yet those monks who were supposed to be your main hosts, sitting in their special seats at the front of the hall, listened indifferently. What kind of behavior is that? I was shocked, so I immediately asked my question. You spoke about the importance of kindness and compassion, but in Japanese society, most people think of monks as people who lack deep compassion. Why is that? And what can we do about it? That is what I asked you. It was a question for you, but it was also a question I wanted to throw out to the Japanese monks in the audience.

I've heard you speak all over the world since the first time I attended one of your lectures seventeen years ago, and I never intended to ask this question first, but I couldn't bear the atmosphere in the hall. Because of the limited time for questions and answers, you only answered the second part of the question. You said that the time when only monks decide how we should practice Buddhism is over, that people from all walks of life—educators, scientists, administrators—should come together to discuss the revival of Buddhism.

After that, in Hiroshima, I asked you a question that went one step further. In your lecture there you spoke about the understanding of emptiness and the practice of compassion. Let me summarize briefly what you said:

The Buddha's teachings have two levels, wisdom and expedient means—or in other words, the understanding of truth and practical action. Wisdom is the knowledge of causality, or emptiness, and expedient refers to nonviolent action, or the practice of compassion. What is emptiness? It is the view that that all phenomena must be understood as mutually interdependent. This idea forms the core of Nagarjuna's teaching of the "middle way." Nothing arises without a cause. In contrast to the Christian belief in a divine creator of all things, in Buddhism we grasp that all things are produced through cause and effect. Happiness, suffering, and all phenomena arise due to specific causes. All things are born not of themselves but from their causes. Causality refers to all things being interdependent, and emptiness is not nothingness, but means that all things exist within causality. All things are empty of self-nature; they do not exist on their own, but are mutually interdependent. You spoke about how in Buddhism both the wisdom of emptiness and the practice of compassion are important.

As I listened to your lecture, I wondered about the connection between emptiness and compassion. Some Buddhist monks understand and expound the doctrine of emptiness, yet clearly lack compassion toward suffering sentient beings, and in Hiroshima I asked you how that situation is possible. You replied that if a person truly understands emptiness then compassion naturally arises, and if it does not, then his understanding of emptiness may be flawed. Emptiness means that all things are interdependent, yet it can be misinterpreted as nothingness. You explained that if we develop our understanding of emptiness, then compassion naturally arises because all things are interdependent and interconnected in causality. Yet I still do not quite understand the part of your explanation about how compassion naturally arises. I think this matter conceals a very delicate problem.

Just as in Shinagawa, many high-ranking monks who attended your lecture in Hiroshima are people who are supposed to have a deep understanding of emptiness, yet they don't seem to develop deep compassion. They made me think that an understanding of emptiness not connected to compassion is a big problem. So I want to ask you the same question again now.

DALAI LAMA: Regarding the understanding of emptiness, there are four philosophical schools: the Sarvâstivāda, Sautrāntika, Yogâcāra, and Madhyamaka. The first two are Hīnayāna philosophies, and the latter two are independent Mahāyāna philosophies; those who study Mahāyāna Buddhism must study all four. The fourth, the Madhyamaka, is further divided into the Svātantrika and Prāsaṅgika schools. To understand profound emptiness, we must grasp the subtle difference among the view of no-self that is emphasized in the Yogâcâra, Svātantrika, and Prāsaṅgika schools. The most profound and highest emptiness, according to the Prāsaṅgika school, is the interpretation that all things exist depending on causes and conditions.

In other words, nothing exists on its own, but rather, existence is understood in such a way that all things arise dependent on causes and conditions. In this view of causality, all things are dependent on other things, and through causality we can perceive reality. Emptiness is understood as causality. When

> *Wisdom is the knowledge of causality, or emptiness. . . . What is emptiness? It is the view that all phenomena must be understood as mutually interdependent.*

we see that emptiness is based on causality, then emptiness does not signify a void in which nothing tangible exists, but rather that all things arise in this world according to cause and effect. My first point is this understanding of emptiness based on causality, in which nothing possesses self-nature. But the mind of compassion does not arise from this understanding alone. This is what your question was about.

My second point is that once we know the meaning of emptiness based on causality, we are able to see that the suffering of all living things is rooted in the mind of ignorance,

*All things are empty of self-nature; they do not exist on their own, but are mutually interdependent.*

and that it is possible to extinguish that igno-rance. Emptiness and ignorance are com-pletely contrary to each other. The failure to understand emptiness and interdependence is ignorance, and as one strengthens one's conviction about emptiness, the mind of ignorance loses its power. Through cultivat-ing this awareness of emptiness, the igno-rance that is the source of our confusion and suffering can be extinguished. We see that sentient beings suffer because of that igno-rance, and a feeling of compassion toward them arises. We become able to see the cause of human suffering. We see that if we extinguish its cause, suffering disappears, and that is how compassion arises.

There are many different levels of understanding of emptiness, but if we correctly perceive the most profound emptiness based on the teachings of the Prāsaṅgika school, then we know that ignorance can be cleared away. When we see sentient beings suffering because of ignorance, the mind of compassion awakens in us.

For monks who study profound sutras and achieve a high level of knowledge, because their knowledge is academic, it is difficult for them to feel compassion toward ordinary

*The failure to understand emptiness and interdependence is ignorance, and as one strengthens one's conviction about emptiness, the mind of ignorance loses its power. . . .*

*. . . Through cultivating this awareness of emptiness, the ignorance that is the source of our confusion and suffering can be extinguished.*

suffering. According to Buddhism, human beings experience three types of suffering: the suffering of physical pain, the suffering of change, and all-pervasive suffering. Of the three, the studied monks tend to be more aware of the more difficult concepts of the suffering of change and all-pervasive suffering than they are of the suffering of physical pain, so when they encounter this "lower" type of suffering it may be more difficult for them to feel compassion. [Turns to Geshe Dorje Damdul.] Do you agree? Why do some people who say they are Buddhists have no compassion? He is right. In Tibet, a grandmother or grandfather who sees a dog that is sick and hungry will feel sorry for it and give it something to eat, while by comparison *geshe* and other monks seem to have no compassion.

GESHE DORJE DAMDUL: Not all monks are that terrible. [Dalai Lama bursts out laughing.] Anyone who has compassion should understand. [The Dalai Lama again laughs heartily.] Really, not all monks are like that. But there are people who lack compassion . . .

DALAI LAMA: [To Geshe Dorje Damdul.] Tell us your personal experience.

He was educated at the Tibet Children's Village School, for Tibetan refugees, where he received a modern Western-style education until he graduated from high school. Then at the age of twenty, he entered our monastery in south India. So he can speak about two distinct educational experiences.

GESHE DORJE DAMDUL: I recognize that some very knowledgeable monks do not translate what they have learned into practice. On the other hand, there are monks who are truly able to use their academic knowledge to cultivate the mind of compassion.

Then their compassion is so transcendent and profound that you cannot compare it with the compassion of ordinary people.

I studied in the monastery for sixteen years, and my personal experience was that monastic life was very different from that of society outside the monastery. In the monastery you felt so relaxed, and your friends were always there to offer you help. But once you leave that institution, then gradually you feel a huge difference, as though there is no one around you and you have to sustain yourself. When I lived in the monastery I felt an enormous amount of harmony, an incredible sense of confidence, security, and happiness.

DALAI LAMA: That's the positive side of it. [Laughs.]

UEDA: You know both sides.

GESHE DORJE DAMDUL: But I do admit there is also a negative side. As you said earlier, among very knowledgeable people in monasteries, some never integrate their knowledge with actual practice, so in spite of all their education and understanding, because of their lack of practice, they may behave in a coldhearted and indifferent way. But there are only a few monks with these negative traits. Most people in the monasteries do integrate study and practice, and many possess deep kindness that is based on wisdom.

DALAI LAMA: In the worst cases, some monks become very learned in monastic institutions, but they are not able to integrate knowledge with practice. They become very eloquent and good at debating other people, so nobody can really challenge them, while in practice they lack compassion and kindness.

*[Three]*

# LOVE AND
# ATTACHMENT

DALAI LAMA: Scientists are already starting to show that inner values [holds hand to his heart] are what matters most for a happy life, and they are what we need right now, not only spiritually, but also for our physical well-being.

Our whole society is deluded by material things and has lost sight of what is truly valuable. We judge everything on a material level, and we don't recognize any other values. In families, too, people who earn money are treated well, and those who don't are treated as useless. People treat their children better if they are likely to earn a lot in the future, and they neglect their children who are not. Some may even feel that since disabled children are not useful it would be better to kill them. The same is true of old people—since they don't earn money anymore they are not treated well and are given nothing but leftovers to eat.

We deal with animals the same way. Hens that lay eggs are treated well, but male chickens are killed. Females that don't lay eggs are also killed. People are exactly the same. Only useful people are valued, and those who are not useful are abandoned.

"

*Our whole society*
*has lost sight*
*of what is truly valuable.*
*We judge everything*
*on a material level,*
*and we don't recognize*
*any other values. . . .*

*. . . In families, people who earn money are treated well, and those who don't are treated as useless.*

UEDA: I completely agree. Your Holiness said that society was youth-oriented, but we can also say that it is use-oriented. Modern civilization recognizes those who are useful, but not those who are useless.

DALAI LAMA: Yes. [Laughs.] Youth is more useful. In a society that treats only useful people well, now we have to pray that we will live shorter lives. [Puts hands together.] When we get old, we will be useless. [Bursts out laughing.]

UEDA: Yes, that's true. It would be better not to live a long time just so we can be abandoned.

*In a society that treats*
*only useful people well,*
*now we have to pray that*
*we will live shorter lives.*
*When we get old,*
*we will be useless.*

DALAI LAMA: Of course, that is not only a Japanese problem. I think most societies believe money is the only way.

UEDA: Money and also social prestige. A son or daughter that goes to an elite school or works for a prestigious company brings the parents a lot of personal pride.

DALAI LAMA: That's right. I think deeper human values and compassionate friends are the most important things in life, but people don't recognize that.

*Deeper human values
and compassionate friends
are the most important
things in life.*

For example, in a poor household that is filled with affection, everybody is happy. But even in a billionaire's household, if the family members are jealous and suspicious and unloving toward each other, then no matter how wealthy they are or how nice their furniture is, they are still unhappy.

This example clearly shows the difference between superficial values and deeper, higher values. The affection and kindness that we human beings originally possess are the deeper values, the foundation of all human values. With this foundation, superficial values that have to do with money and material possessions can contribute to human happiness. Without it, those superficial values are meaningless.

## LOVE VS. ATTACHMENT

UEDA: Would you please explain how we should distinguish between love and attachment? Some parents think that having a "good child" is proof that they are loving parents. They believe that if their child gets into a good school, it is because of their love for the child. Getting into a good school is not a bad thing, of course, but if the parents want the child to get into a good school based on conditional love, isn't that just control that goes by the name of love? Children are not their parents' property, but when the parents treat them like property, that is attachment, not love. It seems they use conditional love to control their children. But what do you think?

They are attached not only to their children, but also to their own image of themselves as the parents of good children. That kind of relationship is not real love.

DALAI LAMA: You very rightly describe it as conditional love and unconditional love. I

*Children are not
their parents' property,
but when the parents
treat them like property,
that is attachment,
not love.*

think genuine love will be given absolutely equally to a bright child or a handicapped child alike. In fact, I think a handicapped child would naturally receive more love, more care. But if the love is not genuine, if it is conditional, then a handicapped child would be seen as useless and would not be loved.

[To Geshe Dorje Damdul.] In Tibetan society is there a difference in parents' love for normal and handicapped children?

GESHE DORJE DAMDUL: As you said, I think handicapped children are loved more.

DALAI LAMA: [In a low voice.] Are they really treated with love? I'm not sure . . .

## HUMANS AND ANIMALS

DALAI LAMA: To some extent I think animals also behave like parents with conditional love. Some kinds of birds give more food to the larger offspring in their nests. I noticed that owls and eagles don't feed the same amount to their larger and smaller offspring. Since they feed more to the larger offspring, I thought maybe the smaller offspring would eventually die. Maybe in the animal world they are distinguishing among their offspring in the same way that humans do. I don't know.

With dogs and cats, puppies and kittens, how do the mothers treat the strong versus the weak offspring? I don't know, but I am very interested in this question. If they are giving more food to the large and strong offspring and not much to their weaker offspring, then they are distinguishing among the value of various offspring. Animals behave in such a way because of biological factors.

Female animals also often prefer males that are larger, so that they will have healthier, stronger offspring. They prefer larger males because of a biological instinct to propagate the species and produce better offspring.

Male deer will often fight over the females, and the one that wins looks majestic while the loser withdraws, looking very disappointed as he leaves. [Laughs.] All these things have a biological basis.

In the same way, if a human mother has several children, treating the stronger child better has a biological origin. And if she sees the weaker child as useless and does not give him very much care—setting aside what we just said about money and a child's value—I wonder if that behavior arises from a biological point of view.

Thanks to your question, I am now very curious. [Laughs.]

Do you think that what we call civilization exists in the animal world? I don't think it does.

UEDA: If culture is a certain fixed pattern of behavior, then we can say that culture exists in the animal world, but civilization is a little more difficult.

In any case it seems that in the animal world the highest priority is the biological impulse to produce offspring. As for human beings . . .

DALAI LAMA: On the animal level, everything is governed by physical factors. On the human level, in ancient times, we were closer to the level of animals, in that physical strength was superior. The physical was all that mattered. But as civilization advanced, human intelligence became more dominant. Through human intelligence, life has advanced and become more sophisticated, and that social development is what we call civilization.

In other words, the concept of civilization is deeply connected to human values, or at least to our intelligence. So the triumph of the strong over the weak on a physical level has become less important.

Intelligence is a very unique trait that human beings possess, and in civilization the intellectual level is superior to the physical level. Just as human intelligence plays an important role, so also do the true affection and kindness that human beings possess.

The most important basic human values of affection and kindness exist on a different level than the intellect. In a civilization founded on the intellectual level, the intellect plays a greater role, and we tend to evaluate and select people based on their usefulness. But if we make only intellectual judgments and neglect our original attributes of affection and kindness, and instead choose and value only things that are useful, there is a danger that we will leave those judgments as the legacy of our civilization. What do you think?

UEDA: Basically I agree with everything you said. From an animal society in which physical strength was dominant, human intelligence gave rise to civilization, which over-came the animalistic law of the jungle. But because the intellect tends to value things according to their usefulness, a different kind of discrimination arose, and by relying solely on our intellectual judgment, we risk sup-pressing the affection and kindness that are our most basic attributes as human animals.

As a cultural anthropologist, however, I would like to add a few comments. Looking back at human history from the perspective of cultural anthropology, it was not always the case that those with the greatest physical strength had the most power. Human society began as a hunter-gatherer society, which historically we know was a perfectly egalitarian society. If a hunter brought in game, the game was divided evenly among all members of the community. In fact, this method is the best one to ensure the survival of the whole community. At that time, of course, game could not be preserved. So, for example, if I shot a big deer and then kept it only for my own family to consume, some would certainly be left over and go to waste. And hunting is a gamble, so that I might catch prey on some days, but other times several days might go by without my catching anything. So the most logical way for the community to survive is that on days that I shoot game, I distribute it evenly among everyone, and on days when others shoot game, they do the same. Because hunter-gatherer societies had this method of even distribution, there was almost no differentiation between people who had power and those who didn't.

But the introduction of farming transformed human society. A farming society is a stationary society, so that people no longer migrated as the seasons changed, the way they had in hunter-gatherer societies. Because hunter-gatherer societies were nomadic, homes were very humble, and it was not possible to save and store things. But farming societies stayed in one place, so that people could now store grain that had been harvested, as well as furniture, household items, and other possessions. In farming societies, the gap between rich and poor expanded dramatically, and a sharp distinction arose between those who had power and those who did not. Social ranks became differentiated; there were now land-owners and peasants, sovereigns and slaves. As the accumulation of wealth became pos-sible and vastly powerful institutions were established, the so-called four great ancient civilizations took shape.

The introduction of farming gave rise to the idea of personal property, so that for survival, instead of dividing resources evenly among all members of the community, it was safer for people to accumulate their own personal resources. Then, in farming societies, people began to fight over power and wealth, and these struggles marked the beginning of systematic warfare. Though in farming societies cooperative relationships among community members were still very important, and to some extent rivalry and antagonism within these communities was stifled, once people began farming, many different social ranks formed, and systematic conflicts arose.

So it is not that the tendency for the physically strong to dominate the weak existed before civilization and was diminished with the advent of civilization; rather, according to the current theory in cultural anthropology, once farming began, power struggles and violence increased.

DALAI LAMA: That's right. But I think even within a hunting society, as with animals, the physically stronger animal takes more meat. When a mother lion kills an animal, the father lion swaggers over [imitates the way a male lion walks], drives away everyone else, and enjoys the meat himself. The strong take more. I think the same was true of early human beings.

UEDA: As a cultural anthropologist, I say no.

DALAI LAMA: Really? But then, compared to other animal societies, human beings have a stronger awareness of community. Everyone's life depends on the community.

*Compared to other animal societies, human beings have a stronger awareness of community. Everyone's life depends on the community.*

UEDA: That is certainly true.

DALAI LAMA: But think about it. A big person naturally has a bigger stomach. Will he be willing to go hungry in order to share with everyone else? I don't think so.

UEDA: You are right, probably not. So the cultural anthropologist is going to agree to some extent with Your Holiness's explanation.

DALAI LAMA: [Happily bursts out laughing.]

UEDA: What you just said made me realize

that I had misunderstood what you meant when you spoke about "civilization."

For cultural anthropologists, civilization began with the four great civilizations surrounding the Nile, Tigris-Euphrates, Indus, and Yellow rivers, and we assume that civilization did not exist before them. So when Your Holiness used the word "civilization," I automatically interpreted it that way. But when you raised the question of whether civilization exists in the animal world, you were using the term in a broader sense, to refer to the system of individual consciousness and society governed by the intelligence in both animals and humans that transcends their animal nature. I just realized what you meant.

In that case, what you are saying agrees completely with my understanding as a cultural anthropologist. The hunter-gatherer societies whose practice of equal distribution I emphasized earlier fall under the cultural anthropologist's definition of "pre-civilization," but according to your definition they are "post-civilization." Hunter-gatherer societies mark a period of history in which a balance existed between the intellect and the basic human values of affection and kindness.

Four or five million years ago, monkeys came down from the trees and began to walk upright and thus took a step toward becoming human. These first humans were called Pithecanthropus, and they were followed by the primitive humans represented by the Peking man and Java man, while human beings today are descended from Cro-Magnon man. These categories do not imply a linear evolution, but they do give a general view of that process. The hunter-gatherer societies I spoke about were already composed of Cro-Magnon man, whose livelihood was hunting and gathering.

What you spoke about as the age in which physically strong people got more food, in which the animal level dominated, corresponds to the age of Pithecanthropus and the primitive humans who followed them. Certainly in the sense that those societies used fire and tools, they were already set apart from wild animals, but human beings were still very animal-like.

After that stage, however, human consciousness evolved rapidly. The brain developed, and brain capacity reached that of human beings today, which led to the awakening of the intellect. For example, when the remains of one of the now-extinct Neander-thal were excavated, it was discovered that he had been living for years with a broken leg. Even though he was disabled, friends had helped him. The age of helping each other had begun.

This period was also revolutionary because the concept of death first arose within human beings. They began to bury their dead. They became conscious of death and the world after death. This awareness was also the discovery of "life." To become conscious of death was to become conscious that they were living life, which was not death. As we came to perceive the basic distinction between life and death, we became more aware that we were alive. The intellect is based on the consciousness that makes distinctions, and the most basic of those is the distinction between life and death.

For a long time, Neanderthal man was believed to be the direct ancestor of the human race, but genetic analysis has disproved this idea. The dominant theory now is that Neanderthal man died out because they could not adapt to various environmental changes. Either way, during this period, the intellect began to develop in human beings, and they moved beyond the stage in which the strong dominated the weak that you spoke about earlier. Hunter-gatherer societies were based on mutual help and even distribution of resources.

To sum up this history of the human race, the "civilization" you spoke about and the hunter-gatherer societies I referred to both belong to a period when human beings transcended the dominance of strong over weak, and they came to possess the intellect, but still held onto the basic attributes of affection and kindness. With the shift to a farming society, however, people planted seeds in spring and harvested crops in autumn, and thus became aware of time. As the intellect became dominant, people increasingly made distinctions based on usefulness, and the intellectual violence of those who killed others in their quest for wealth and power became acceptable. Yet farming societies still had a powerful sense of community, which suppressed the maladies caused by the intellect. With the rise of industrial societies, however, the power of the community declined, and people forgot that they were social animals. Because we mistakenly began to see ourselves as individuals living separate lives, it was no longer possible to stop the reckless domination of the intellect. Then our most basic human attributes of affection and kindness became obscured.

## LOVE AND
## INNATE HEALING POWER

UEDA: Was it good for the human race to develop the intellect? We are not merely animals, but animals that possess an intellect; this intellectual capacity has produced civilization, but it has also brought us a lot of suffering.

*Most of our spiritual problems are due to our very sophisticated intelligence and powerful imagination.*

DALAI LAMA: Yes, that's right. Most of our spiritual problems are due to our very sophisticated intelligence and powerful imagination. Science and technology have also given us unlimited hopes. As a result, we sometimes forget our basic nature as human beings.

UEDA: Our basic nature as human beings.

DALAI LAMA: Yes—our basic nature as human beings, which comes from our basic nature as mammals. Let's take the modern medical system as an example. When a person is sick, Tibetan medicine generally seeks to bring forth the body's inherent natural healing power. But Western surgical procedures seek to cut out the part of the body that is not working, as though repairing a machine. Once a machine breaks, it cannot repair itself. So with a machine, the broken part must be taken out and thrown away. But our bodies are not machines. Even if the human body is damaged, sick or hurt, it has the inherent natural power to heal itself. When we rely too much on modern science and technology, our lifestyle itself becomes like a machine, and we move away from our basic human nature.

*When a person is sick, Tibetan medicine generally seeks to bring forth the body's inherent natural healing power. But Western surgical procedures seek to cut out the part of the body that is not working, as though repairing a machine.*

*. . . But our bodies are not machines. . . . When we rely too much on modern science and technology, our lifestyle itself becomes like a machine, and we move away from our basic human nature.*

A person who has become like a machine has no room left to cultivate affection or compassion for others. We are all knowledge, but we lack compassion.

UEDA: This idea is very interesting to me, because my first research as an anthropologist was on the mind-body connection and the theme of the body's natural healing power. In my late twenties, I lived in Sri Lanka for two years, where I studied the power of folk Buddhist exorcism rituals to heal the sick. These exorcism rituals are very lively events that involve the whole village. For people who do not get well in the hospital, or those who suffer from depression or lethargy, the village holds a ritual vigil that heals the sick person through dancing and laughter that bring everyone together. The interesting thing is that in Sri Lanka people believe that evil spirits tend to possess those who are lonely. They say, "Lonely people attract the gaze of evil spirits." When others look at us with kindness, then evil spirits can't get to us, but when other people ignore us or harbor malicious feelings toward us, then evil spirits can strike. In this exorcism rite, the villagers come together to support the patient, be together, laugh together, and the

*A person who has
become like a machine
has no room left to
cultivate affection or
compassion for others.*

warm compassionate gaze of the villagers is what heals the lonely patient.

Why does this exorcism heal people? When I returned to Japan, I started to explore the fields of mind-body medicine and immunology. I became interested in neuroimmunology, the scientific discipline that was not yet widely known at that time and that deals with how a person's mental state influences the immune system and the body's innate healing power. I became aware that scientific investigation was starting to demonstrate the reality of the forces I had seen at work in these exorcism rituals.

When we cooperate with each other, when we are connected through mutual trust, when we are filled with love and compassion, the immune system is strong. But when others betray us or we feel neglected, when we feel angry and sad at the way others have treated us, the power of our immune system declines dramatically. The feeling of loneliness combined with powerlessness weakens the immune system more than anything else. When we feel alone and abandoned but cannot do anything about it, when love and compassion have abandoned us, the body's defenses are at their lowest. Then we can get

*Fear, anxiety, and stress*
*weaken the immune system.*
*Some scientists have*
*described anger as eating*
*our immune functions. . . .*

*. . . On the other hand,*
*a relaxed state of*
*compassion and kindness*
*brings us inner peace and*
*supports and augments*
*the function of the*
*immune system.*

"

sick easily, or an illness like cancer that the immune system has been keeping in check can surge out of control. Science has already shown that our mental and physical health are deeply connected.

DALAI LAMA: What you say is a very powerful argument for the importance of peace of mind, compassion, and kindness. In an industrialized society like Japan, it is not sufficient to study Buddhist teachings and texts. We need efforts to link those teachings to scientific knowledge. Fear, anxiety, and stress weaken the immune system. Some scientists have actually described the anger as eating our immune functions. On the other hand, a relaxed state of compassion and kindness brings us inner peace and supports and augments the function of the immune system.

These scientific facts demonstrate the importance of inner values to people in modern society. These inner values cannot be produced by medicine, injections, or machines. The only way is for us to realize how important these values are and to make the effort to cultivate them. The important thing now is to investigate these ideas in our own mental laboratory, especially whatever has to do with the emotions.

For that purpose, the Buddhist tradition offers very rich resources. Buddhism categorizes the different emotions and explains in detail how to deal with negative emotions and increase positive ones. Then Buddhism becomes relevant in our daily life.

[*Four*]

# ENLIGHTENED BUDDHISM FOR A MODERN WORLD

UEDA: Buddhism is not just about chanting sutras, but is also connected to the scientific knowledge we spoke of earlier, about the connection between the immune system and an inner state of kindness. What is the meaning of Buddhism today, and how can it be made relevant for modern society? It must not remain a closed religious world, but must be brought into daily life.

DALAI LAMA: There is a saying, "Whatever you do, if it is not accompanied by enlightenment then no matter how many mantras you chant, you will be reborn as a snake."

The mind of enlightenment is not mere knowledge, but an innate mental quality. We feel and experience it deep within ourselves. Ceremonies, prayers, mantras, and chanting sutras are not sufficient. Reciting the Heart Sutra in itself is no different from playing a tape recorder [laughs] if it is not accompanied by the enlightened mind.

UEDA: You certainly know that the Japanese people like the Heart Sutra and that there are unenlightened priests who chant like tape recorders. But some people say that reciting that Heart Sutra has magical powers. I really

*The mind of enlightenment
is not mere knowledge, but
an innate mental quality.
We feel and experience
it deep within ourselves.
Ceremonies, prayers,
mantras, and chanting
sutras are not sufficient. . . .*

*. . . Reciting the Heart Sutra in itself is no different from playing a tape recorder if it is not accompanied by the enlightened mind.*

do feel that the sounds of the sutra's words hold something mysterious.

DALAI LAMA: I think in some special circumstances, just hearing the sound itself has good effects. [To Geshe Dorje Damdul:] Would it help animals too? Even if an animal did not have the karma for it to produce good effects, do you think that listening to the sutra would help him?

GESHE DORJE DAMDUL: I think hearing the sutra would help that animal only if he already had the karma for it to produce good effects.

DALAI LAMA: To become a tathāgata [literally, "thus come one," an epithet for a Buddha], one must have accumulated both virtue and wisdom. Both must be there. It is the same thing.

To bring Buddhism to life, we must have a Buddhist revival. To do that, Buddhism must be thoroughly explained on the basis of scientific research. I think that's the proper way to do it.

UEDA: So Buddhist doctrine itself should be changed or amended?

DALAI LAMA: No. There is no need to rectify or change Buddhist doctrine.

UEDA: Then what must be changed? Buddhist doctrine itself does not need to be changed. Then is it an attitude or something else that we have to change?

DALAI LAMA: First, the Buddhist community should have a deeper knowledge of how the Buddhist system works. And then this practice should be thoroughly researched according to scientific findings, so that it becomes real and convincing.

Then monks should guide other people in the study of Buddhism. That is why the monks themselves must first pay more attention to the importance of study. Through religious practice, the monks should serve as examples of good human beings. If the monks can truly be examples for others, then people will be led to study and practice Buddhism.

So these changes are nothing new. This is not reform, but revival.

# THE BUDDHA'S SPIRIT
# OF SOCIAL SERVICE

UEDA: Buddhist teachings take human suffering as their starting point, and today we must also begin by asking what kind of suffering we now face. When monks just deliver their sermons, prepared in advance with no attention to people's actual suffering, then they may talk about Buddhism, but their way of explaining it is not Buddhist. Their approach is far removed from Śakyamuni's original desire to save people from suffering.

DALAI LAMA: In the 1960s I had the opportunity to visit Thailand several times. On one occasion I spoke with the supreme head of Thai monastic Buddhism, the Sangharaja, and I said to him, "Our Christian brothers and sisters work very sincerely for the good of society, in education, medicine, and welfare. We Buddhists traditionally lack those activities, but I think we should learn some of those practices from our Christian brothers and sisters." But the Sangharaja told me, "No, we Buddhist monks should remain isolated from society." It's true. The Vinaya sutra says that monks should remain isolated from society. But that does not mean we should avoid any useful or beneficial engagement in society. The Vinaya says that a monk should live in a peaceful place, isolated from worldly people, keep the monastic rules, and follow a pure way of life, but that does not mean he cannot engage in service to society, including social work, welfare, or education.

The Buddha himself is a good example. One day he noticed a very sick monk whose body was dirty because no one had looked after him. So the Buddha himself brought water and poured it over him, and asked his disciple Ananda to wash the sick monk's

*The Buddha did not only
preach but also acted.
That is truly social service.
Like Jesus Christ, we
followers of Buddha must
have the same spirit of
helping the sick and the poor
and working on behalf of
modern education.*

body. The Buddha did not only preach but also acted. That is truly social service. Like Jesus Christ, we followers of Buddha must have the same spirit of helping the sick and the poor and working on behalf of modern education.

In Thai monastic tradition monks can live according to the Vinaya sutra, isolated from worldly life, but they should also emulate the Buddha's own charitable activities. Both aspects of religious life should be correctly understood and combined. The rule that says Buddhist monks and nuns should be isolated from worldly society does not mean that they are prohibited from doing any kind of social work.

UEDA: I agree. In daily life they should remain separate from worldly life and secure a sacred space for monastic practice, but they should also have a compassionate spirit and be actively involved with society. That is the best way. Recently even in Thailand, with its Hinayāna tradition of striving for self-liberation, a small but growing number of monks are getting involved with social action.

> *Buddhist training is based on the practice of karuna, or compassion. And compassion must be implemented in the form of social service. That's very crucial.*

DALAI LAMA: [Surprised.] In Thailand? I didn't know that.

UEDA: Beginning in the 1970s, some Thai monks started to practice social action. They are known as "development monks," and they are involved in activities like building hospices for AIDS patients and developing reciprocal aid programs for helping the poor. As you said, the mainstream of the Thai Buddhist establishment still remains separated from worldly activities, so only a few monks are involved in social work.

DALAI LAMA: I have heard about monks

involved with environmental issues. But in general I don't know much about it. In any case, our Christian brothers and sisters are much more active in social service. And what about the Hinayāna Buddhists in Sri Lanka?

UEDA: Sri Lanka has the famous Sarvodaya movement.

DALAI LAMA: I do know about that.

UEDA: The movement was founded by a young high school teacher named A. T. Ari-yaratna and takes Buddhist teachings as its foundation while advancing the cause of farming development in a dynamic way. It has grown so much that it has become one of the leading NGOs [nongovernmental organizations] in the world. Now that I think of it, though, Sarvodaya is a lay movement, not a monastic one.

DALAI LAMA: Buddhist training is based on the practice of karuna, or compassion. And compassion must be implemented in the form of social service. That's very crucial.

UEDA: Some forward-thinking Japanese monks who have visited Thailand have been astonished and moved to see the compassion of the Hinayāna Buddhist monks there expressed as support for AIDS patients and other social projects. Of course, since Japanese Buddhism is a Mahāyāna tradition, we tend to look down on the traditions of Thailand and Sri Lanka as Hinayāna, or "Small Vehicle" Buddhism, that seeks only individual liberation. Yet these Hinayāna Buddhist activities show that it is a much bigger vehicle than the "Great Vehicle" of Japanese Buddhism. Japanese monks come back from Thailand very surprised, because even with all its talk of the Bodhisattva's practice for the salvation of all beings, Japanese Buddhism is really the tradition with the small vehicle. In some cases, those experiences do also inspire social action in Japan.

DALAI LAMA: I see. Some Hinayāna Buddhists engage in compassionate action. But many Japanese temples or monasteries also run schools. That is wonderful too.

UEDA: Yes. Many temples have schools and kindergartens. These institutions could truly serve as places for cultivating compassion and kindness.

# Self-Responsibility
# in Buddhism

DALAI LAMA: Guru yoga is very important in the Tibetan tradition, but one negative aspect of it is that guru yoga emphasizes the attitude of entrusting everything to the guru, which leads to the danger of too much dependence on the guru.

Someone once asked me what it means to take refuge [in the Three Treasures of Buddhism: the Buddha, dharma, and sangha]. The question was whether taking refuge means to become perfectly dependent on something, to lose your independence. But in Buddhism, especially in the Mahāyāna tradition, taking refuge means that we aspire to become like Buddha ourselves, and in that act, individual pride is very strong and we do not become dependent.

In religions that accept the existence of God, however, everything is created and determined by God. God is great, but I am nothing.

UEDA: I hardly exist at all.

DALAI LAMA: In that way of thinking, the self cannot act autonomously, because we are perfectly dependent on the creator God, and God determines everything. This way of thinking is very useful for some people, but from a Buddhist point of view, it discourages people from having self-confidence, pride, the creative power to accomplish things.

The Buddha taught that ultimately you yourself should become a Buddha. And he himself was once an ordinary person like us. He set an example for us by practicing until he attained Buddhahood.

UEDA: Your point is very clear. According to Buddhism, it is not that God determines

*The Buddha taught that*
*ultimately you yourself*
*should become a Buddha.*
*And he himself*
*was once an ordinary*
*person like us.*

everything, but we ourselves create the world; Buddhism is a teaching that begins by strengthening individual subjectivity.

Now I understand what Your Holiness meant yesterday when we spoke about competition, and you said that to take refuge in the Three Treasures is to embrace a spirit of rivalry with the Buddha and the sangha. To take refuge in the Buddha does not mean to entrust everything to the Buddha, but to embrace a positive spirit of rivalry with the Buddha, to declare our own determination to become Buddhas. That act brings out the power latent in me, so that I have the pride, compassion, and kindness to improve myself and act in the world. At times I may have compassionate anger, and I will abandon attachments that must be abandoned, but I will hold tightly to the Bodhisattva's attachment to relieving the suffering in the world.

## TRANSCENDING SUFFERING

UEDA: I would like to ask Your Holiness about the middle path. When you spoke at the international Buddhist conference in New Delhi in 2004, I was struck by how you emphasized the importance of the middle path. Many high-ranking monks had gathered together for this big international conference, and Your Holiness told them that the middle path is very important in Buddhism, but it does not simply mean staying in the middle, avoiding extremes. The Buddha himself was born as a prince and enjoyed a life of worldly pleasure in the palace, and then renounced the world and went to live as an ascetic far from human civilization, where he practiced fasting and austerities until he nearly died. Even through those ascetic practices, he did not attain enlightenment, so he came out of the forest, healed his mind and body, and then entered into meditation and attained enlightenment. You said that the middle path means avoiding extremes of pleasure and pain, but it does not mean that we should merely remain in the middle from the start.

Sometimes we go to the places where people are suffering to experience what they are going through firsthand, and other times we seclude ourselves quietly in a monastery. In Buddhism, the true meaning of the middle way is moving dynamically between the two, experiencing both. I was very impressed with your talk in Delhi, because so many monks and other Buddhists do not address the actual problem of suffering, but mistakenly think that the middle path means just to sit comfortably in the middle, avoiding extremes, without doing anything.

In the same lecture you said that we were all gathered there for the cause of world peace, but you asked if we thought peace was important because the Buddha taught that it is, or because we ourselves were deeply convinced that we must do something to help the situation in the world. You said that it is not enough to want peace just because the Buddha taught that peace is important.

Your Holiness said that no matter how much we have personally experienced the horror of violence, unless we are convinced of the need for peace, it means nothing to go around merely repeating that the Buddha taught peace is important. You said that it is not enough to remain quietly meditating in the monastery—we must confront the violence in the outside world.

DALAI LAMA: It is foolish to say that the middle path means to be indifferent to reality or not even to know about the other extremes.

The Buddha taught the need for peace. Naturally we may ask why he taught that peace is important. Why?

We know that violence causes suffering. So we may seek peace because we think that to get rid of that suffering we must put an end to violence. We need to have both the Buddha's teachings and the awareness that is based on our own actual experience.

If we look at the Buddha's life story, it is clear why he taught the middle path. The Buddha himself taught based on his own experience. He started out as a young prince from a wealthy household, who was very spoiled and was not aware that after birth human beings experience old age, sickness, and death. Blessed in every way, the Buddha never imagined that he himself would get old, get sick, and die, but when he actually went out of the palace and saw the lives of the people in the town, when he saw the sick, the old, and the dying, then for the first time he understood that reality. He was astonished when he saw for himself people that were experiencing the suffering of birth, old age, sickness, and death, when he realized that sooner or later he too would experience those things. Then, for the first time, he became aware of the reality of human suffering. He abandoned his wealthy lifestyle and his position as a prince, renounced the world, went off alone to undergo religious training, and practiced austerities for six years.

During that period, he often fasted, but he ultimately realized that fasting and other physical efforts were not sufficient. He saw that he had to use his intelligence, so he stopped his ascetic practices and began to eat again. When he used his intelligence to cultivate wisdom, then for the first time, he attained enlightenment.

*Even without trying to,*
*sooner or later we all*
*experience suffering and*
*want to put an end to it.*
*To eliminate suffering, it is*
*absolutely essential to use*
*our human intelligence to*
*cultivate wisdom.*

All of the Buddha's teachings are based on his own experience. First, we must become aware of suffering. Even without trying to, sooner or later we all experience suffering and want to put an end to it. To eliminate suffering, we must understand that ascetic physical practices are not enough, but that it is absolutely essential to use our human intelligence to cultivate wisdom. The Buddha himself taught based on his own experience, and we too must start with our own experience of suffering.

Other religious leaders say the same thing. For example, Jesus Christ went through many difficulties and suffered terribly, and in the end he was crucified. But I think the teaching of Buddhism is more precise and more human in its approach to suffering.

# AFTER
# THE INTERVIEW

The interview ended with the Dalai Lama bursting out laughing at one of my jokes. He laughed and laughed. It was a fitting conclusion to the two days of interviews, a great burst of energy.

From beginning to end, the room in which we spoke was filled with energy, regardless of whether we were silently absorbed in thought, expressing anger and indignation, listening intently to each other's words, or bursting out laughing together. No concluding words were necessary. All of us in the room knew that every moment of the discussion was filled with deep meaning. And we were all sure that we had to share this material with many people by publishing it.

When the Dalai Lama stood up, he placed a white ceremonial scarf, called a *kata*, over my shoulders and blessed me. Then he took my hand again and led me outside to the courtyard so we could have photos taken there.

In the courtyard, although it was December, a few flowers bloomed here and there. It was a wonderful garden, filled with sunlight. Released from two days of intense concentration and filled with a sense of satisfaction from the conversation, I felt blissful as I walked in the garden with the Dalai Lama holding my hand. When we took the pictures, he again grasped my hand and did not let it go until the session had ended and we had gone back inside.

"We'll see each other again," said the Dalai Lama, when he finally let go of my hand as we stood in the corridor facing the garden.

"I want to make our conversation into a good book," I said. "And I look forward to seeing you next year in Japan."

"Good! Thank you!" said the Dalai Lama, and he smiled as he turned to go into the living room. As I stood watching him go, my heart overflowed with gratitude. Without even realizing it, I put my hands together and bowed to him.

When the Dalai Lama reached the door to the living room, he turned and put his hands together in farewell, smiled, and disappeared through the door. Even after he was no longer there, I still stood there for a little while with my hands together.

When I came back to the presentation room, the Dalai Lama's English translator, Geshe Dorje Damdul, and his secretary, Tenzin Taklha, were waiting for us.

"It was really an amazing interview. I am very grateful to you," I said, and Geshe Dorje

Damdul replied in the same sincere voice as during the interview: "The topics you asked about and discussed were things that the Dalai Lama had wanted to talk about for a long time. That's why he was so happy when he was talking to you."

I promised to meet the two of them again and bid them farewell. On the way back to the hotel, we were all filled with a sense of satisfaction.

"The Dalai Lama's face was really wonderful. A face like no other in the world. And it was a magnificent conversation, filled with energy," said Mr. Ōmura, the cameraman, whose excitement from the meeting had not yet subsided. Those admiring words from a veteran photographer who was constantly on the road photographing monuments, Buddhist images, and ordinary people's lives throughout Asia, who was known to every Asia researcher, expressed how we all felt. Mr. Ōmura had happened to be in Delhi for a different photo shoot, and he came to photograph our conversation at the last minute. An expert Asia traveler, he arranged a car for us that would be sure not to break down on the road in the middle of the night, personally went to buy us thick blankets to protect us from the cold, and generally acted as the guardian deity of our trip.

Maria Rinchen [who translated the Dalai Lama's words into Japanese during the interview] too spoke with a mixture of surprise and excitement. "I think His Holiness felt that someone had come from Japan with whom he could really talk," she said. "As much time as I have spent with him as his translator, I have never seen him like that before."

Anyone would have felt happy to be part of that conversation. We had all shared a rare experience.

The interview was over, but the work was not. As soon as we got back to the hotel, we started working on the translation of the second day's interview. I knew that if I let too much time pass, later I wouldn't be able to understand the figures of speech and context of the conversation. Our plan was to finish a first draft of the manuscript in Dharamsala. As we worked intently on the translation, it grew dark outside.

We continued the work the following morning and finished just before noon. For us, the interview with the Dalai Lama had now really ended. As we enjoyed a leisurely lunch in the hotel restaurant overlooking the valley, I felt that I could finally relax. During the interview, I had given myself over to the energy of that space, and I was absorbed in every moment of the conversation. But during our work on the translation, I became aware of many new things.

The interview had ended with a burst of laughter, but the Dalai Lama had carefully brought closure to the conversation. He had said that not only people were exploited, but also animals. I remembered that at the beginning of the conversation he had murmured the same word, "exploitation." This interview began and ended with "exploitation." Even as monks talk about helping other people, in fact, they are eating them up. The Dalai Lama was keenly aware of the evils to which religious people can succumb. If he used his own authority and power in the wrong way, he could cause great suffering. He was very aware of that fact.

That's it, I thought. During our interview, I never heard the Dalai Lama invoke his own authority or power. He never talked down to me. As young and inexperienced as I was, he always spoke to me as an equal. We debated as equals, happily discovered new ideas, talked about how to build a better future. His lack of self-importance made such a free-flowing conversation possible.

Some people criticize the Dalai Lama because he is not only a religious figure but also a political one. Of course since he is the "sovereign" of Tibet, which now faces such tragic circumstances, and he seeks to restore its peace and autonomy, naturally he is active in politics. In our interview he emphasized the social nature of Buddhists; he said that Buddhists should participate responsibly in society, and that while dedicating themselves to religious practice, it is only right that they should also help those who are having difficulties in life.

Even religious people who say monks should not involve themselves with social issues but should remain indifferent to politics are themselves sometimes extremely political. They behave in an authoritarian way, they lead people into discussions that they can dominate, they show off their greater knowledge and authority, and they encourage people to become their followers. They say monks should not get involved with politics, yet they are passionate about politics within the religious community, and they spend a lot of money to win internal elections. They distinguish their monastic ranking by the color of their clothing and fight to be promoted to higher ranks.

They have no social awareness or interest in other people's suffering, yet they love internal politics, and they are eager to rise within the ranks of their religious institutions. And once they have reached a high position, they flaunt their power and authority and use it to control others. The Dalai Lama is fully aware that unless a religious person disciplines himself, he can easily fall into that kind of corruption. That is what he calls "exploitation."

"Exploitation" is a harsh word. Yet because the word implies self-discipline, it is also a source of freedom. I think the emergence of the word "exploitation" at the beginning and end of our interview was not unrelated to the freedom and warmth of our conversation.

I had spent the past two days in the hotel and the Dalai Lama's residence. Now at last I had time to walk around the town of Dharamsala. Yet my feet carried me once again to the Dalai Lama's residence. His home and Namgyal Monastery are located on a small hill encircled by a path around its perimeter. A trip around the path takes only about thirty minutes, but it is a holy path where you will always find pilgrims who have come to visit Dharamsala.

When I descended the slope to the left of the entrance to Namgyal Monastery, I soon came to the entrance of this path. It is a small path that is easy to miss. I followed the road clockwise, with the hill with the Dalai Lama's palace and the temple on my right. The sky was clear, without a single cloud. Behind me off to the left was the Himalayan mountain range and ahead I could see far across the Indian landscape. It was warm out, and I took off my sweater.

On a stone outcropping along the way, some Tibetan characters were carved into the rock. They spelled out *oṃ maṇi padme hūm*, Avalokiteśvara's mantra, the words people chant as an expression of deep gratitude for the Bodhisattva's compassion. Each letter of the mantra was painted a different bright color—white, green, yellow, red, and blue—and as I walked along I felt strangely intoxicated by the sight of them. A few minutes later, as I stopped again before the letters, a group of Tibetans came along, but they paid no attention to me. It was noon on a weekday, so many of them were older people. At some points along the path, there were large and small prayer wheels. Spinning several hundred prayer wheels with *oṃ maṇi padme hūm* inscribed on them while circling the path is supposed to have the same effect as chanting several hundred mantras. In this way, people recite countless mantras, with their voices and by spinning the prayer wheels, as they circle the perimeter road.

About midway along the road there was a clearing with a *stupa* (a tower that houses Buddha relics) built on a little hill. When I climbed the steps to the stupa, I could see the landscape opening out in all directions. To the right were the Himalayas and to the left countless prayer flags fluttering in the wind. The prayer flags, called *lungta*, were also brightly colored, white, green, yellow, red, and blue. The scene was like something not of this world. Then I heard the sound of a voice reciting a sutra. When I turned to look, I saw a young monk, probably still in his teens, sitting halfway up on the hill, reciting a sutra. He seemed to be memorizing something for an examination, walking around as he concentrated, repeating it over and over again. It was very picturesque to see this young monk reciting a sutra beside the stupa, with countless colorful prayer flags fluttering in the wind and the majestic Hima-layas rising in the distance.

This was obviously a holy place. It was the holy land of Avalokiteśvara. In the middle of this circular path dwelled the embodiment of Avalokiteśvara, the Dalai Lama. It was a peaceful day. The sky was absolutely clear, and the Himalayas glowed brilliantly in the sunlight. These were people of deep faith. Nothing was missing. Holy time flowed through a pure space. I spent a few blissful minutes beside the stupa.

And yet . . . during that blissful time I suddenly realized that there was definitely something missing. There were the shining, towering Himalayas, but the Tibetans' homeland was on the other side of them. All of these people were refugees who had crossed over the Himalayas. So was Avalokiteśvara himself.

## THE DALAI LAMA'S SOCIAL ACTIVISM IN INDIA

After we had gone once around the circular path, we visited the Tibetan Children's Village (TCV), a boarding school for Tibetan refugee children that was located about four kilometers outside of town. There are seven TCV schools in India, and the school in Dharamsala serves as their headquarters. Fifteen thousand children, from infants to age eighteen, are enrolled at TCV schools, with 2,500 at the school in Dharamsala.

Why a boarding school? Because most of the children's parents are still in Tibet. There are also many orphans. Each year more than 400 children make the journey across the Himalayas from Tibet as refugees. Some come with their parents, while in other cases the parents entrust their children to other refugees for the border crossing, while they stay behind in Tibet. Often parents may bring the children across the border, drop them off, and return to Tibet without them.

Why do these parents send their children into exile, even if it means being separated from them? Because in Tibet, the Tibetans themselves are poor and do not have access to a proper education. No education based on traditional Tibetan culture is available to them. Many parents want their children at least to receive a Tibetan education, so they send them into exile. But it is a harsh journey. Even adults die from the cold when crossing the Himalayas. They must walk for more than ten days, fighting hunger and cold. There is also the border patrol, who will mercilessly shoot even children. As the deeply moving documentary *Escape over the Himalayas* shows, even when the children have made it across the border alive, they still sob for their mothers. These are the children that come to the Tibetan Children's Village.

Yet this children's village was an extremely cheerful place. From there the sweeping view of the Himalayas against the blue sky was even more brilliant than in town. The buildings were much nicer than I had imagined, though the interiors of the dormitories and classrooms were so humble that a Japanese student would probably be shocked. Most importantly, the children were healthy and happy. Of course, because they were children, there were a few fights and quarrels, but just by looking at them, you could tell where their energy was focused. This place was filled with the love and kindness that the Dalai Lama spoke about. Children of all ages, from preschool to high school, are raised to take care of each other like brothers and sisters.

The educational level at the school is also very good. About half the graduates go on to study at Indian universities. The universities in India are much more difficult to get into than those in Japan. In fact, Maria's three children attended this refugee school, even though it was a six-kilometer walk from where they lived; now two attend the American school and one the British school. I met Maria's oldest daughter when she came to Japan; she is now studying medicine and is very excited to become a cardiologist. It makes me wonder about Japanese education. Why do we send our children to cram schools from a young age and make them study so hard for exams, without cultivating the inner qualities of affection and compassion? Why do we spend so much money to educate our young people, just for them to end up with an inferiority complex, no dreams, and no academic ability?

The cheerfulness of the refugee school has much to do with the Dalai Lama's cheerfulness, I thought. All the children are unfortunate: They cannot depend on their parents who are so far away. They may never return to their homeland. Yet they are fortunate: they study hard, grateful to their parents who, though far away, wanted to give them the best education possible, and grateful to those who support them here. And they are extremely cheerful.

This refugee school was founded by the Dalai Lama's older sister, Tsering Dolma, as a foster home for children, and after her death, their younger sister, Jetsun Pema, succeeded her. The Dalai Lama's whole family is active in society. They have tackled the difficult job of taking in refugee children who are mentally and physically exhausted and mourning the separation from their parents who are far away.

# THE WINGS OF FREEDOM

After my interviews with the Dalai Lama, I found out something that surprised me. On the morning of the second day we met, before our interview in the afternoon, he had had an audience with a group of refugees that had just arrived in Dharamsala from China. These were people who had risked their lives to cross the Himalayas, holding the image of the Dalai Lama in their hearts, unafraid of the cold or altitude sickness or the danger of getting shot. Many of those who survive the crossing have to have fingers or toes amputated because of frostbite. Some collapse and fall ill when they arrive. First they are treated at a refugee receiving center in Nepal, and once they have recovered their strength, they travel in groups of several dozen at a time to Dharamsala. There they meet the Dalai Lama, whom they have dreamed about all their lives.

That meeting had taken place the morning of the previous day. It must have been such an overwhelming moment for the people who had just arrived. They must have been deeply moved in a way that we cannot begin to imagine.

My interview with the Dalai Lama had been squeezed into his schedule at the last minute. Two days later, he was to travel to the holy site of Bodhgaya to give a dharma talk to a crowd of thousands of people. His secretary, Tenzin Taklha, had told me that these were the only two days the Dalai Lama had available for the interview, but he had really fit me into a very tight schedule. That effort reflected the Dalai Lama's own strong desire to meet with me, and I had no words to express my gratitude.

I can only admire the strength that allowed him to grant such an interview after meeting the refugees that same morning. The refugees must have been trembling with emotion. Yet behind that emotion there was surely great sadness. Who would go into exile if he were happy? Their families had been killed and tortured; they had faced poverty and despair. Sustained only by the hope of exile, they had to risk their lives to cross the border. The Dalai Lama knows their sadness. He knows their suffering. He absorbs it with his whole being.

He confronted their sadness and pain, all the absurdity and cruelty they had encountered. Yet a few hours later he spoke so freely and creatively and became completely absorbed in a childlike curiosity. He changed his mindset and feelings so dramatically, laughing heartily as he talked with me. How did he do it? How could he make such a switch? Most people would not have been able to do it.

Yet it wasn't an emotional switch. The morning and afternoon were connected. He himself has experienced sadness, suffering, the absurdity and cruelty of this world. He shares the others' pain, and he groans with them. He feels the same anger and outrage. That anger motivates him to find the causes of suffering in the world and to work harder in his own religious practice, so that he can confront that suffering directly and enlighten humanity, so that without exploiting himself or others or resorting to violence, he can help create a society that will bring freedom and happiness to all people.

The experience of pain and sorrow leads to enlightenment and a deep wish for salvation. A great desire for freedom emerges. To go from pain to limitless freedom is Buddhism. That is the path the Buddha himself took.

# Salvation for All

During my interview with the Dalai Lama, I realized for the first time what it meant that he was the living embodiment of Avalokiteśvara and why he exists in the first place.

It is well known that the Dalai Lama reincarnates in successive human forms. When a Dalai Lama passes away, a search party forms to look for the next Dalai Lama, and they travel all over Tibet seeking the child that is his next incarnation. The fourteenth Dalai Lama was discovered at the age of three as the reincarnation of the thirteenth Dalai

Lama. The reincarnating Dalai Lama is also the embodiment of Avalokiteśvara. When Avalokiteśvara's life as a human being ends, he appears again in a different human form.

From a Japanese point of view, all this sounds exotic, and for Westerners even more so. When I first saw the Dalai Lama in person at that international conference seventeen years ago, the Western participants there gazed at him with a fascination for the "mystery of the East" that he represented to them.

But why does the Dalai Lama reincarnate? Why does Avalokiteśvara bodhisattva manifest himself? Many people say it is because

Tibetan society believes in reincarnation. All living things reincarnate, and so does the Dalai Lama, so do bodhisattvas. But only the Buddha escapes from the cycle of birth and death. Life is suffering, and reincarnation is the continuation of suffering. Only the Buddha escapes from rebirth and suffering and attains the liberation of nirvana.

Yet Avalokiteśvara reincarnates because he wants to. Avalokiteśvara is the bodhisattva who vows to Amida Buddha that he will save all sentient beings. He is the bodhisattva who saves sentient beings for countless eons until at last he attains enlightenment and Amida invites him to become a buddha. But Avalokiteśvara turns down that offer. He says, "I want to be attached to helping sentient beings. I will not become a buddha, I will keep coming back as a bodhisattva until I have saved all beings from suffering.

"Instead of attaining liberation and becoming a Buddha, I want to keep being reborn and saving sentient beings . . ."

The Dalai Lama is not simply being reborn. The bodhisattva's will to save sentient beings from suffering is manifested in the form of the Dalai Lama. He emphasizes positive attachment that is worth keeping because he himself is the manifestation of Avalokiteśvara's own attachment. Without the attachment to saving all sentient beings, the Dalai Lama would not exist. That will is what gives birth to the Dalai Lama. I felt that keenly throughout our interview. There is a will that precedes birth and death. There is a will that precedes existence. That is what a bodhisattva is.

But Avalokiteśvara does not merely reincarnate so that he can inherit an old tradition. To save sentient beings, Buddhism must change with the times. A bodhisattva must strive to continuously learn, learn, learn. He must deeply study the old traditions as well as modern society and modern science. He must seek ways for traditional Buddhist teachings to meet the demands of modern society, and he must continually investigate the role of Buddhism in his own time. If he does not, he cannot really save anyone.

The Dalai Lama himself must feel deeply how powerless Buddhism is when it does not keep up with the times, how powerless a bodhisattva is when he cannot address the society in which he lives. This is how he describes his youth in Tibet in *Freedom in Exile: The Autobiography of the Dalai Lama* (New York: HarperCollins, 1991): "Of course, whilst I lived in

Tibet, being Dalai Lama meant a great deal. It meant that I lived a life far removed from the toil and discomfort of the vast majority of my people. Everywhere I went, I was accompanied by a retinue of servants. I was surrounded by government ministers and advisors clad in sumptuous silk robes, men drawn from the most exalted and aristocratic families in the land. My daily companions were brilliant scholars and highly realized religious adepts."

When he was a child, regents who were sometimes corrupt or sought personal benefit held the real political power, and because they lacked foresight and ignored the revolution that had occurred, they ended up allowing the Chinese invasion to happen. Buddhist teachings could not stop the invasion either. This sense of powerlessness is expressed clearly in the Dalai Lama's autobiography.

No matter how profound a teaching is, if it does not keep up with the times, it has no power to help those who are suffering. The Dalai Lama must have felt powerless, but he did not allow that feeling to dominate him. As Avalokiteśvara, what could he do to alleviate human suffering? At that time, he cast off the husk of the person he had been until then.

He stopped reigning from the top of a pyramid, where the only people he spoke with were those who worshiped him. To test out the logic of Buddhist teachings, he began to have discussions on an equal footing with scientists, politicians, and other religious leaders. He put himself in situations where he might lose arguments, as he groped for what role Buddhism could play in the world. That approach is exactly the opposite of the attitude of religious people who also feel powerless but never engage in debate unless they are sure to win and be able to show off. Buddhism was not there to feed the Dalai Lama's power, but only to help humanity.

When we hear that the Dalai Lama is the living embodiment of Avalokiteśvara, we tend to think that idea belongs to an old outdated tradition. Yet it is because the Dalai Lama is the embodiment of Avalokiteśvara that he is on the cutting edge of modern society. When he visited Stanford University in 2005, he spent one day of his three-day program there in a symposium with pioneering neuroscientists from the medical school, engaged in a wide-ranging discussion with them on the topic of how desire, attachment, and suffering arise. The Dalai Lama actively engages in dialogues with today's leaders all over the world.

His lifetime of over seventy years spans feudal times, modernity, and post-modernity. He was raised as a feudal monarch, yet in exile he has promoted the modernization of politics and religion. In place of the coldness of the modern social system, he advocates a society that is based on affection and kindness. This affection and kindness does not merely represent a revival of traditional values. It is not a movement to restore what has been lost, but to manifest the affection and kindness that have developed in the wake of modernization, that are right for our times.

Avalokiteśvara, whose life spans from feudal to post-modern times, is none other than the Dalai Lama himself.

# ACKNOWLEDGMENTS

This book came to be with the support of many people. I would like to offer my thanks to them here.

Kawahara Eishō, head priest of the Shingon Ritsu special sectarian headquarters Renge'in at Tonjōji, is the person who first introduced me to the Dalai Lama. Mr. Kawahara, who has dedicated himself to international volunteer efforts, has a deep respect for the Dalai Lama and invited him to give a lecture and symposium at Renge'in in Kuma-moto prefecture in 2005. Inspired by my book *Reawakening Japanese Buddhism,* he said that he would like to help arrange for me to interview the Dalai Lama and proceeded to write the Dalai Lama several letters. Without his work behind the scenes, this interview would never have taken place. I offer my sincere thanks to the exceptionally active, bold, meticulous, and passionate Mr. Kawahara.

Representative Chope Paljor Tsering and Lungtok of the Dalai Lama's offices in Japan gave me their thoughtful consideration, communicated with the Dalai Lama's government offices on my behalf, and presented me to His Holiness in Japan. "A project that is based on a good inner motivation will certainly be realized," Representative Chope told me, and I am very happy that the result of this project has lived up to his words. I also want to express my sincere thanks to the Dalai Lama's secretary, Tenzin Taklha, for setting up everything perfectly for the interview, and to Geshe Dorje Damdul for his kind support.

The person who made the travel arrangements for India was also the photographer who provided the wonderful pictures for this book, Ōmura Tsugusato. Mr. Ōmura is highly knowledgeable about India, and without that sturdy and distinguished blanket that he bought for me, I would not have gotten a wink of sleep, and I don't think I would have made it to the interview. Maria Rinchen of Dharamsala also provided a clear Japanese translation of the Dalai Lama's words. With her practical knowledge and lovely smiling face, Maria cheerfully provided support for us during the interview. During the breaks from our intensive work, I heard about Maria's life trajectory, which is so unique that everyone at the meeting said she should write a book about it, and I certainly hope she will write it.

I owe my ability to conduct this interview with the Dalai Lama in English, a project I would have hesitated to undertake before, to the students at Stanford University. Over the course of twenty lectures on the topic, "Can Buddhism Respond to Contemporary Problems?" they patiently endured my poor English and engaged in an active discussion with me, and that experience gave me the ability to conduct this interview. I also want to thank my good friend Michael Zimmermann (now at the University of Hamburg), the associate professor who invited me to co-teach the course with him, and also Carl Bielefeldt and

Bernard Faure (now at Columbia University) for hosting me so kindly at the Stanford Center for Buddhist Studies.

Finally, above all I would like to thank the Dalai Lama. I don't know how to express my gratitude to him for giving me the chance to interview him and for generously offering so much of his time and energy to this project. I hope to convey his message to the Japanese people and work to cultivate true affection and compassion in Japan. I hope that I can honor the Dalai Lama's blessing by continuing to talk to the world with compassionate anger about peace. I sincerely pray for the

Dalai Lama's health and for freedom and peace in Tibet, and I will be strongly aware of Japan's responsibility to the world as we look toward the future.

—June 1, 2007

# ABOUT THE AUTHOR

Noriyuki Ueda is a well-known Japanese author, lecturer, and cultural anthropologist. In 2006, he was a visiting research fellow at the Center for Buddhist Studies at Stanford University where he taught a 20-part series, *Buddhism Today: Responses to New Global Challenges*.

# Hampton Roads Publishing Company

*. . . for the evolving human spirit*

Hampton Roads Publishing Company publishes books on a variety of subjects, including spirituality, health, and other related topics.

For a copy of our latest trade catalog, call (978) 465-0504 or visit our distributor's website at *www.redwheelweiser.com*. You can also sign up for our newsletter and special offers by going to *www.redwheelweiser.com/newsletter*.